Walking By the Homeless

Laura E. Sandretti

Orange Hat Publishing
www.orangehatpublishing.com - Waukesha, WI

For information, please contact:

Orange Hat Publishing
www.orangehatpublishing.com
603 N Grand Ave, Waukesha, WI 53186

The author has made every effort to ensure that the accuracy of the information
within this book was correct at time of publication. The author does not
assume and hereby disclaims any liability to any party for any loss, damage,
or disruption caused by errors or omissions, whether such errors or omissions
result from accident, negligence, or any other cause.

www.orangehatpublishing.com

To the young man who taught me to be present with people instead of walking past them. A young man, who by all statistics, should have turned out the exact opposite of the joyful, thankful, trusting, and loving person he is. Foley, you've opened my eyes to so many things and taught us all so much. You are in our hearts, lives, and prayers . . .

Forever.

TABLE OF CONTENTS

FOREWORD

Father Douglas Leonhardt, S.J., recently reminded me that being a Christian is a remarkable privilege *and responsibility*: being the heart and hands of Jesus Christ on earth. Think about that—doing His work on this earth, being His representative on this earth.

As Laura notes in this wonderful work, faith without action is dead. We accept the privilege and fulfill the responsibility of Christianity by sharing our talents and gifts with those in need as God calls us to do.

God calls us in mysterious ways. Seldom, I suspect, does He call through Jim Stingl, columnist in the *Milwaukee Journal Sentinel*, who wrote an article about a young boy who needed adopting. But one day He did. Laura and her family listened, and the life of a child with a special place in my heart has been tremendously enriched. In like measure, Laura and her family's life (and my life and my family's life) has been enriched by our relationship to this child. There is privilege in Christian responsibility.

This book will help you listen for God's whispered call: to know it can come at any time or place, through any medium— or no medium at all. This book has helped me listen. I am more than confident it will help you, too, and motivate you to answer that call.

Christopher R. Foley
Milwaukee Circuit Court Judge

Introduction

This is the story of my journey from being comfortable, complacent, and compartmentalized in my finances, marriage, parenting, and faith to being uncomfortable, challenged, and different. This is a story to help women like me—suburban, Jesus-loving, family-oriented, well-intentioned individuals— discover how to cultivate a lifestyle of service. This is a story meant to move us beyond good intentions, regret, and a feeling of helplessness when it comes to serving the poor in spirit in our inner cities and in our country clubs. This is a story about what I have learned helping broken people: in my living room, in the scary neighborhoods not-too-near but close enough to where I live, and the one staring back at me in the mirror.

This is a story about how to do *something*, in Jesus' name.

It was not my passion to help the poor and marginalized. I did not desire or seek out the homeless—I ignored them. My journey also did not begin when I looked romantically into the middle distance inspired to do greater, more significant things. I did not have time to do anything more than I was already doing. My path began where I was currently living life. It began first with my own head, heart, and home. God began orienting me toward the people He cares about in the way He always does, by teaching me more about Himself by teaching me more about myself.

This book is as much about a shift in my faith in Jesus Christ as it is about how I went from ignoring the homeless to identifying with them. This book is about learning to serve in Jesus' name, but it is also about debunking the hopes, subconscious ideals, and expectations that being a Christian happens quickly, easily, or magically. I wish there was a definitive event, Bible verse, or sermon that led to a deeper awareness and understanding about the areas in which God, in His love, wanted to transform me, but there was not. God works in my life as He does in everyone's, by calling us to be faithful with the little, unglamorous, and mundane things before we are entrusted with anything bigger.

Being a "good-Christian," I had prayed regularly for years, studied the Bible, attended church every Sunday, and taught women at conferences and moms' groups about God's Word. However, it was not until the Holy Spirit began opening the eyes of my heart—while I was doing an in-depth study of the book of Luke—that I began to realize the magnitude of disconnectedness in my life: the disconnect between the wife and mother I was and wanted to be and the disconnect between the passionate faith I wanted but did not have.

I also began to become aware of the disconnect between my educational, spiritual, and financial wealth and my attitude and response toward the poor. Although the six months I spent studying Luke began my journey of transformation in many areas, it would be years before what I was learning manifested itself with the homeless. Becoming who we want to be, serving more faithfully and compassionately, and growing in our faith depends on what Gregory Boyle calls aptly, "the slow work of God."[1] But

---

[1] Boyle, 128.

it is in that slow work God helps us learn and change.

What I have learned in the past several years, and continue to learn, is how easy it is to be selective about my commitment, obedience, and beliefs. I am learning it is sometimes more desirable to help others than stay home and help my marriage. I am learning that looking at others with pity and compassion does not translate into anything of value or help without seeing myself and others as made in the image of God.

What I have learned about helping the poor was that until I learned more about myself and my faith in Jesus Christ more deeply and *uncomfortably*, I was unable to begin being the woman I wanted to be inside or outside the walls of my home. God, in His love, has been helping me for the past five years reexamine my marriage, family, and priorities in a new light. In the process, I became better able to serve more effectively, faithfully, and with greater longevity once He opened my eyes to the poor and homeless.

This book can be read at your leisure, cover-to-cover, or as a six-week devotional. There are six chapters, each containing five sections. One section can be read daily Monday through Thursday with a "To Ponder" question to reflect on after each reading. Friday's section has a passage to read and a prayer challenge. You will find out in the book that I am addicted to efficiency, so nothing in this book is long, but it is meant to take you deeper. If you do nothing else after you read, I hope you will accept the prayer challenges at the end of each of the chapters. They are short, but sweet!

With the exception of my family and a particular Mr. Charles Wiggins, whose name I felt I could not modify, give anonymity to, or fail to include, most names have been changed to protect and respect people's identities. It is my genuine hope and prayer that this book makes you, above all else, think. *Walking By the Homeless* is not meant to guilt anyone into service; rather, it is meant to help readers see where God is already at work in your heart, home, and with the homeless, so you can join Him in doing your small something, too.

CHAPTER ONE:
BEFORE YOU GO

"I do believe,
help me overcome my unbelief."
Mark 9:24b (NIV)

I remember a few years ago reading *The Hiding Place* by Corrie Ten Boom, and although I knew Corrie was a Holocaust survivor, I did not know much else about her life. I was eager to read the book I had heard so much about. The first half of *The Hiding Place*, however, contained details, the backstory about Corrie's childhood, her father's love for the Bible and the Lord, and other particulars leading up to and impacting the rest of Corrie's story. Unfortunately, I am not patient with backstories, not Corrie Ten Boom's, my own, or anyone else's. However, I am learning that backstories are pivotal. Without a backstory, we never get to a climax. Without a backstory, we do not learn, grow, or arrive. Before I could do "something" for the homeless, I needed a backstory to lay the foundation I would need in my mind, heart, and home to serve well. This chapter is my backstory.

Part of my backstory, which is still being written, was identifying and distinguishing my beliefs. Part of what helped me begin to transform in every area of my life, including with the homeless, was learning to distinguish among what I say, think, and really believe, the difference between abstract and core beliefs. Timothy Keller differentiates between abstract and what I call core beliefs by identifying abstract beliefs as logical and core beliefs as experiential. An abstract belief is one we "assent to with the mind but have not grasped with the heart."[2] A core belief, conversely, is one that moves us to action.

Abstractly I believe that God is more powerful, wise, and loving than anyone. Based on the amount of stress I experience trying to control my schedule, life, and outcomes, however, it is not a core belief. Abstractly I believe, and have told my children, that my husband is the head of our household. The core belief I live and act out of, however, is that I make most of the decisions regarding our children, rules, and calendars. Abstractly I believe it is important to help the homeless, but since my typical response toward the homeless was to ignore them, it was not a core belief.

The difference between abstract and core beliefs is not necessarily bad or something to be ashamed of. However, they are something to recognize and confess, like the man in Mark's gospel who believed *in part* Jesus' power and ability to heal his son. As I become more aware of the discrepancy between what I say and want to believe and the core beliefs that motivate my actions, the more I pray about, grow, and change in the places where God wants to deepen and strengthen my faith. The more I can allow the Spirit to work in me and speak to me through God's Word, the more abstract beliefs will become truly real to my heart.

Jonathon Edwards illustrates the difference between abstract and core beliefs with this analogy:

---

[2] Keller, 170.

"Thus there is a difference between having an opinion that God is holy and gracious and having a sense of the loveliness and beauty of that holiness and grace. There is a difference between having a rational judgment that honey is sweet and having a sense of its sweetness. A man may have the former that knows not how honey tastes; but a man cannot have the latter unless he has an idea of the taste of honey in his mind."[3]

Keller says, "We do not live as we should – not because we simply know what to do but fail to do it but rather because what we think we know is not truly real to our hearts."[4] Abstractly believing and knowing Jesus' love has prevented me from serving and loving others with any degree of consistency or depth. However, the beauty of understanding the difference between abstract and core beliefs is that this understanding begins to reveal disconnectedness. Becoming aware of the difference between abstract head versus core heart beliefs is the difference between living an examined life and not really living at all. Although I realized some of these discrepancies existed, I did not know how far the gap was between who I was and who I wanted to be.

To PONDER: What is a belief you have about Christ that does not move you to act? Do you believe there is no condemnation for those who are in Christ Jesus but find yourself frustrated and angry with yourself when you mess up (again)? Do you believe in the saving grace of Christ but, like me, are not bold enough to tell your non-Christian friends about Him?

---

[3] Ibid., 163.
[4] Ibid., 164.

. . . .

American Idols

"To whom will you compare me?
Or who is my equal?" says the Holy One.
"Lift your eyes and look to the heavens:
Who created all these?
He who brings out the starry host one
by one and calls them each by name.
Because of his great power and mighty strength,
not one of them is missing."
Isaiah 40:25-26

Another part of my backstory was learning what motivated me to ignore the homeless in the first place.

God does not work like I do. He does not compartmentalize, have a checklist, or "fix" me in one area and then move onto the next. When I look back on the many months I spent studying the book of Luke, I realize that although one of the main themes in Luke's gospel is about the poor, it is also about all the things we put before God. Although the Spirit began speaking to me loudly through the book of Luke about helping the poor, God first wanted to reveal to me, in His love, the idols I was subconsciously putting before Him.

I struggle with concepts in the Bible, such as idolatry, that seem antiquated and irrelevant. When I think of idolatry, I usually think of Aaron and the golden calf incident from Exodus or voodoo dolls from the *Gilligan's Island* TV show I watched growing up. I dismiss idolatry being a personal, prevalent, or prominent threat. However, a big part of my journey to a lifestyle of service was recognizing where I struggled with idolatry in the same way the Israelites did. It was seeing how putting my children, efficiency, and free time alongside God as my most important priorities was thwarting a lifestyle of service.

In the Old Testament, an idol was a copy representing a god or gods.[5] Idols were things in the Old Testament that were burdensome, temporal, and did not help when trouble came.[6] Being consumed with ensuring the wellbeing, success, and safety of my children was incredibly enslaving and burdensome for both my family and myself. Trying to find my worth in what I got accomplished in a day and how my children turned out was fleeting and frustrating.

My little gods had another thing in common with Old Testament biblical idolatry, too. Most religions during the time of Moses consisted of a pantheon, or collection, of gods, "a divine assembly that ruled the realm of the gods, the supernatural and ultimately, the human world."[7] When Exodus 20:3 warns, "You shall have no gods before me," it was not referring to other gods being before Yahweh; rather, it was prohibiting Israel from viewing God among a host of gods or even as the head of other gods.

In the months leading up to and during my in-depth study of Luke, I began to realize that my core beliefs revealed some idols. None of my idols were egregious, illegal, or unethical, however, and I loved God, read and studied His Word, and even taught my children and others about Him. Yet He was at best the

---

[5] Bromiley, 202.
[6] Kohlenberger, 456-57.
[7] Keener, 195.

head of and among the things and people I loved, trusted, found pleasure in, and put my hope in: my children, my to-do lists, and my leisure.

The danger of modern idolatry is that it looks subtle and well-intended, and it is usually accepted and encouraged by everyone around us, just as it was in ancient times. Being a good mother is not bad or egregious by any standards, including biblical ones; however, idolatry is not just about avoiding what is bad. Idolatry is putting our hopes, dreams, and joys into something or someone other than God. Although I had quit my job as a high school teacher to be fully vested in the raising of our three children, parenting became an obsession. I poured my life into raising what I hoped, though not consciously, were not only well-mannered, on-the-honor-roll, and church-attending children, but children free from suffering, pain, and hardships.

Although I began to realize my children were where I was finding my identity and worth, I believed I was doing what was best, and I abstractly believed God was still my first love, priority, and pleasure.

"IDOLATRY IS putting our hopes, dreams, and joys into something or someone other than God."

Modern Christian idolatry is also subtly dangerous, because it has the appearance of something good. I was raised by my strong, industrious Japanese mother and my hard-working, ex-farmer, and ex-military father. How could the Asian Hillbilly offspring of that kind of dynamic duo fail to be anything less than efficient, motivated, and busy? Idle time was not only frowned upon, being caught doing nothing came with ramifications. My worth and value became inextricably linked with my accomplishments, so time and my to-do lists were what I valued most. My desire to control my schedule and ensure that I did not waste time became something I was burdened and enslaved by. Although I became increasingly irritable and infuriated when someone interrupted or forced me to change my plans, I had no idea that productivity and controlling my calendar had become idols.

Idolatry also preys on emotions. Around the time I began my study of Luke, by the grace of God, my kids were doing well in school, socially, and in their faith life. I was doing a satisfactory job managing my career and family while continuing to pursue my master's degree in seminary. God had provided my husband a job that more than amply provided for us financially. After years of raising our children, going to school, enduring my husband's travel schedule, and going through two corporate job relocations, we could finally breathe. However, breathing evolved subtly into leisure, which evolved into a lifestyle justified by entitlement. We had worked hard for years and *deserved* our leisure. Relaxation, travel, and enjoying our limited free time became something we coveted and valued. Because we had earned it, it never crossed my mind that it had become an idol.

Although children, the ability to work, and having the resources to enjoy life are gifts and blessings from the Lord, as I studied the book of Luke, I slowly began to wonder, *So what?* I began to question what I was teaching my children by sending them to private schools, giving them a privileged life, and trying to ensure that life was not too hard, painful, or challenging.

Was that the goal of Christian parenting? Had I been successful, and, if so, by whose or what standards? Did my full calendar without room for margin to love people who interrupted my plans reflect the gospel? Was working hard so we could vacation and relax every free weekend the pinnacle of what we had strived to accomplish? In His love, God began allowing me opportunities to see and grow uncomfortable with my idols to help me see more of myself, Himself, and the people around me.

To PONDER: What do you love, trust, and find pleasure in regularly more than you do God? Discovering our idols is not for condemnation. It is meant to free us from the bondage of idolatry, so do not be afraid to answer. The answer can help start to set you free!

••••

A BLACK FRIDAY WAKE-UP CALL

"With the tongue we praise our Lord and Father,
and with it we curse men, who have been made in
God's likeness." James 3:9

Idolatry was not the only place the Lord, in His love, wanted me to be released from before sending me outside the walls of my home. Another big part of the backstory that led to my involvement with the homeless was my marriage. For over twenty years, I was the wife I did not want to be. The ramifications of my idolatry with my children and obsession with being efficient and constantly in control began to adversely manifest themselves more and more in my relationship with my husband. Being in control gave me the illusion or perception I was invincible and untouchable. I am a sensitive individual and had been hurt in relationships in the past. Being in charge in my marriage, I suppose, subconsciously made me feel less vulnerable to getting hurt again. Although I was aware and even felt badly about being bossy, demeaning, and even manipulative, I never seemed to be able to change. My husband, a quiet, placid engineer who thinks in numbers, was helpless against my tirades. I was aware of my shortcomings. However, despite my feelings of regret, trying to follow instead of lead, and speaking about marriage and parenting in my role as women's director and as a Christian public speaker, I continued business as usual, not realizing the magnitude of the damage I was doing.

Until one Black Friday as I was beginning my study of the book of Luke.

The abbreviated backstory was I had gotten mad at my husband, Chris, while we were doing a little Black Friday shopping with our kids. I had accused him, in my usual sarcastic and belittling way, of making a poor parenting decision. Chris explained why he did what he did, and as we headed toward the exit, I came to the humbling and awful realization that I was wrong. When we got in the car, I admitted my mistake and apologized; however, my husband made almost no response. We coexisted for several days, exchanging pleasantries devoid of emotion. If you have been married longer than five minutes, you understand the dynamic when you cannot resolve an argument, but you have to still live in the same space. Finally, my husband told me he did not accept my apology because he was not upset about *what* I had said. He did not accept my apology because he was upset with the tone, sarcasm, and disrespect with which I had said it. He was so upset, in fact, that after twenty-one years of marriage, he said to me he did not know how much longer he could live with me talking to him like I did.

Sometimes God lines everything up. He allows situations and lessons to point us toward a pattern of sin, dysfunction, and destructive behavior because He loves us. He loves us so much He sent Christ to set us free from, among many things, the disappointment we are to ourselves. Often, if you are like me, you say and believe you want your husband to be the disciplinarian and spiritual leader of your home. However, when the opportunities present themselves for God to help you with what you have asked for, they are unappealing and difficult—so unappealing and difficult we often end up missing out on the opportunity for any change to take place. I would ask God to give Chris the desire to lead and take a more active role in parenting our children, but when Chris would finally muster up the courage to do what I had prayed for, I would correct, belittle, or chastise him, and then wonder why God was not answering my prayers.

The Black Friday incident, dreadful as it was for everyone, woke me up. Although my husband assured me repeatedly he was committed to me and to our marriage and did not intend to go anywhere, his comment shook me. He did not know how to live being talked to the way I spoke to him too often. He felt defeated and exhausted, and I finally realized I had left him no choice. Despite feeling bad and wanting to change for over twenty years, hearing my mild-mannered husband say he did not know how to function being spoken to the way I had for so long impacted me dramatically. I knew I had to begin to more fully surrender to the wife the Bible taught me to be if I was ever going to become the wife Chris and I both wanted me to be.

Whenever God sanctifies us and helps us look more like Christ, the process is slow and painful. Jesus said, "If anyone would come after me, let him deny himself and take up his cross daily and follow me" (Luke 9:23). It is rarely fun to deny ourselves, but when we see the hurt we cause those we love, it becomes easier to ask God to show us how to surrender our "rights," responses, and control issues over to Him.

What do idolatry and a Black Friday showdown have to do with my journey from the suburbs to the inner city? Decompartmentalization.

God does not compartmentalize or separate faith from our everyday lives. He provides opportunities in the people and situations right in front of us to answer our prayers. God uses our backstories. He did not call me into obedience with the marginalized in Milwaukee without first calling me to obedience in my heart and home. I had to recognize my children and calendar for what they were: idols equal to God and the reason for my safe, sanitary, and sporadic service. God began helping me see where I had been arrogant, disobedient, and ignorant in my marriage, so I could not only become the wife I wanted to be more often, but so I could learn what biblical humility and sacrifice looked like all the time. He allowed me the opportunity to become aware and begin fixing the mundane, everyday issues inside me so I could be more effective with greater longevity outside my home. The Lord wanted to free me from idolatry, self-centeredness, and a life of abstract beliefs to move me beyond good intentions in every area of my life.

To PONDER: What every day relationship is difficult for you right now? Are you the wife, daughter, mother, friend, and sister you wish you were?

• • • •

UNREST

"Whoever can be trusted with very little can also be trusted with much . . ." Luke 16:10a

The most effectual and overriding part of my backstory, the one that led to my eventual walk alongside the homeless, was a shift in my relationship with the Bible. The book of Luke was one I had read many times, but this time was different. Slowly and almost imperceptibly as I read, studied, and wrote papers on the book of Luke, I had the relentless sense that there were more disconnects. Luke's gospel began to consume and convict my heart and mind quietly, constantly, and uncomfortably, not only about my marriage and idols but also about my educational, financial, and spiritual place of privilege. Although we had sponsored a Compassion International child, befriended and hosted an Indian missionary couple, taken my family to the Milwaukee Rescue Mission on Christmas Day, and participated in other isolated events that I crossed off my mental and spiritual to-do lists, they were exactly that. The security, predictability, and convenience of my service began to feel very uncomfortable, but worse than that was the realization of my complacency about it all.

It is easy for me to read my Bible to check it off my to-do list. People like me who thrive on efficiency often can also thrive more on completion than processes. I had read Luke many times, but this time I had to read it slowly and unpack it. Studying Luke for a grade forced me to read with intention rather than merely for completion. As I read Luke, the word "poor" in particular seemed to jump off the page into my heart and mind as if under a microscope. Jesus, early in his teaching ministry, says,

> "The Spirit of the Lord is on me, because he has anointed me to proclaim good news to *the poor*" (Luke 4:18a). Jesus tells John's friends, ". . . Go back and report to John what you have seen and heard: The blind receive sight, the lame walk, those who have leprosy are cured, the deaf hear, the dead are raised, and the good news is preached to *the poor*" (Luke 7:22). In Luke 14:13, Jesus instructs, "But when you give a banquet, invite *the poor*, the crippled, the lame the blind . . ." (italics added).

The more I read and the more I was becoming aware of my idols and abstract beliefs about the underprivileged, the louder verses like Luke 8:14 seemed to speak directly to me, "The seed that fell among thorns stands for those who hear, but as they go on their way they are choked by life's worries, riches and pleasures, and they do not mature."

2 Corinthians 7:10 talks about the difference between worldly and godly sorrow. Godly sorrow is "God-centered sorrow over the wickedness of sin;"[8] conversely, worldly sorrow "is at best a

---

[8] NIV Study Bible, 1771.

shallow remorse, but which is consumed by bitterness and self-pity . . ."[9] Although there have been times in my life and faith walk that I have felt pressure to serve out of guilt or—equally as misappropriated—felt good about myself because I did help, I began to experience godly sorrow as I read the book of Luke. I did not feel condemnation or shame; rather, I simply began becoming aware. Condemnation for those of us who love and believe in Jesus Christ is never from the Lord (Romans 8:1). The Holy Spirit was highlighting the gap between my comfortable, safe life and what the Bible said about my educational, material, and social wealth, but He did so in love, not in shame. It is important that when we read the Bible or about someone's journey to help the marginalized, we are not motivated out of guilt. God highlights disconnects in our lives always out of love.

My timely, in-depth study of God's Word in the book of Luke stirred something in me. I did not know it at the time, but I was growing increasingly uncomfortable. Looking back, that unrest was God preparing me for something and, more importantly, for someone. Every good work God has already prepared for us is never a project, list, or situation. God's business is always about people. He is always about relationships. Toward the end of my study of the book of Luke, after the Lord revealed to me areas of disconnect in my heart and home, I read about a twelve-year-old, inner-city orphan named Foley. God, always in His love, began to show me another area where my abstract beliefs did not line up with my actions.

---

[9] Barnett, 135.

To PONDER: Is reading the Bible a checklist activity, like it was for me for twenty years, or do you enjoy reading it? Do your actions line up with your answer? For example, if you enjoy reading it, are you reading it daily, and do you look forward to reading it? Remember, deciding if a belief is an abstract or core one helps us grow and is not an exercise in shaming or condemning what we do or fail to do.

• • • •

Chapter One:
Before You Go —
Putting It All Together

READ ROMANS 8:1-17

Therefore, there is now no condemnation for those who are in Christ Jesus, [2] because through Christ Jesus the law of the Spirit who gives life has set you free from the law of sin and death. [3] For what the law was powerless to do because it was weakened by the flesh, God did by sending his own Son in the likeness of sinful flesh to be a sin offering. And so he condemned sin in the flesh, [4] in order that the righteous requirement of the law might be fully met in us, who do not live according to the flesh but according to the Spirit.

[5] Those who live according to the flesh have their minds set on what the flesh desires; but those who live in accordance with the Spirit have their minds set on what the Spirit desires. [6] The mind governed by the flesh is death, but the mind governed by the Spirit is life and peace. [7] The mind governed by the flesh is hostile to God; it does not submit to God's law, nor can it do so. [8] Those who are in the realm of the flesh cannot please God.

[9] You, however, are not in the realm of the flesh but are in the realm of the Spirit, if indeed the Spirit of God lives in you. And if anyone does not have the Spirit of Christ, they do not belong to Christ. [10] But if Christ is in you, then even though your body is subject to death because of sin, the Spirit gives life because of righteousness. [11] And if the Spirit of him who raised Jesus from the dead is living in you, he who raised Christ from the dead

will also give life to your mortal bodies because of his Spirit who lives in you.

[12] Therefore, brothers and sisters, we have an obligation— but it is not to the flesh, to live according to it. [13] For if you live according to the flesh, you will die; but if by the Spirit you put to death the misdeeds of the body, you will live.

[14] For those who are led by the Spirit of God are the children of God. [15] The Spirit you received does not make you slaves, so that you live in fear again; rather, the Spirit you received brought about your adoption to sonship. And by him we cry, "Abba, Father." [16] The Spirit himself testifies with our spirit that we are God's children. [17] Now if we are children, then we are heirs— heirs of God and co-heirs with Christ, if indeed we share in his sufferings in order that we may also share in his glory.

REFLECT

Romans 8 has always confused me. I could not reconcile that I could be controlled by the Spirit but still gossip about my neighbor, angrily and repeatedly cut people off in traffic, and ignore the homeless. A commentary on Romans helped me begin to reconcile this tension, however. Grant Osborne explains what Christ has already done on the cross *"launches sanctification,"* not perfects it[10] (italics added). When we realize and accept Christ's love and death for us, God, like in a court of law, *declares us immediately holy.* Our legal standing before God has been decided; we are innocent. Our thoughts, actions, and words, here and now, however, are in still the *process* of being conformed to our legal standing. Becoming who we wish

---

[10] Osborne, 197.

we were (but how God already sees us because of Christ) takes time. Discovering our idols, moving our beliefs from abstract to core ones, and learning humility is something the Spirit leads us in. We just must learn to hear Him better. But how?

PRAY

So much of my journey from complacency to change in my faith and life and with my urban neighbors came from prayer. However, over the last five years, I have learned I talk more about praying than praying. I think more about people, problems, and things than I pray. My mind wanders down rabbit holes of distraction and problem-solving rather than talking to God and letting Him solve them. Why?

Because I only abstractly believe in God's power, ability, and willingness. I abstractly believe my prayers will do something. I abstractly believe He will act. How do we move from a place of only going through the motions of prayer? How do we come alongside the Holy Spirit to cooperate with Him in turning our abstract beliefs about prayer into core ones? How do we pray differently, with greater passion and more expectation?

Part of learning to pray and hear more, better, and more meaningfully is to practice praying. Actually praying. Spend two minutes praying about your questions, doubts, and struggles with prayer. Turn your phone off, close your laptop, and ignore the dog and the voices in your head for two minutes and ask God your questions, tell Him your frustrations, apologize to or thank Him. Just pray.

CHAPTER TWO:
THE DISCONNECT

"In the same way, faith by itself, if it is not accompanied by action, is dead." James 2:17

The story of how I went from walking past the homeless to walking alongside them would be better if it were not so long and mundane, but, again, the Christian life and call to a lifestyle of service is not glamorous, romantic, or easy. What I hope my life in Christ will look like and what it really looks like reminds me of my son learning to play the drums. He wanted to look like Animal on *The Muppets* after one lesson; instead, he had to learn over the course of many hours and boring lessons how to hold a drumstick, where to hit the drum, and what height his stool should be. Although this is the edited version of how we got involved with an inner-city child named Foley, there were many repetitive, often dull and difficult, details that led to and were a part of this journey. There were times I was mad at God about how He answered, failed to answer, or was slow in answering my prayers. More than once, people assigned motives to my involvement with Foley that I felt were inaccurate and hurtful, and there were times along the way I doubted if I had heard from God.

The edited version of the exciting parts of our lives can be interesting, but they are not the whole story. God works best in the long, uninteresting, and seemingly silent moments of everyday life. The boring, arduous times of waiting make up more of my story with Foley than parts I will highlight here, but it was in the waiting where I was forced to listen and learn. It was in the difficult times of waiting that I understood more about hearing the Holy Spirit and what obedience looks like. In the waiting, I began to understand that I was abstractly serving in Jesus' name but subconsciously expecting ease, personal glory, and a worldly definition of success.

One morning, after filling rice bags for people in Tanzania with our church, I was convicted again about how sterile, sporadic, safe, and self-serving my service had become. I realized I did not mind helping until I did mind it. I complained when the doors were locked when we arrived to help. I complained when we went to get coffee (while waiting for the doors to open) and could not find a Starbucks. I did not want to wear a hairnet to fill the rice bags. I look like a 12-year-old Asian boy whenever I wear anything on my head, and I am vain enough to care. I felt they should have selected someone else with power tool experience to seal the rice bags. Fear of those bags popping open before they even left the country haunted me for days. When I finally heard my mental and verbal complaints (we are always the last to hear ourselves), I was embarrassed and appalled. As I often do when I need to vent, I wrote a blog post,

> "God works best in the long, uninteresting, and seemingly silent moments of EVERYDAY LIFE."

repented, and asked God to help me adapt a lifestyle of service that was not pretty, predictable, or even particularly desirable.

Although the Lord had been working in my heart and mind as I studied Luke that semester, literally the morning after I wrote the blog post asking God for something I wanted—and believed abstractly—I read about an African-American orphan whom a local judge was trying to help get adopted. Despite the fact that thousands of people probably read that article, when I read it, I felt everything I had been convicted of and learning about in Luke in the past six months had become reality in the form of opportunity: an opportunity I wanted nothing to do with mostly because it impacted my time and family idols head on.

The moment I started reading about the young man, I got a pit in my stomach, started choking up with tears, and was filled with anxiety. I can unequivocally say I had never before (or since) had such an extreme, immediate, and horrifying response to a newspaper article. I knew I needed to start praying . . . but for whom? I innately find it very difficult to pray for someone when I do not know that someone's name. I realize full well I should not name anything or anyone, lest I become attached to it, but this was too big, too scary, and too important. I needed a name. Without really thinking about it, I started calling the boy "Foley." Christopher Foley was the name of the judge in the article, so "Foley" it was. I began that day, and almost every day since then, praying for and about "Foley."

Our most well-intended, heartfelt, and passionate prayers, however, often become overshadowed and consumed by what we can see. Faith often and easily can be drowned out by the fear of what is in front of us. Despite my education and experience as a former high school special education teacher, how could I consider bringing a child—who was on medication, had a plethora of cognitive and behavioral labels, and had lived in an institutional setting for almost his entire life—near my three children under the age of fourteen? Although I had training, education, and experience working with emotionally and behaviorally disturbed teens, I was not sure this was smart or safe. My husband was also understandably concerned about our involvement with Foley. My husband, who rarely said no to much of anything, said no, and conversations about our involvement with Foley were causing stress in our relationship. The Black Friday incident was still fresh in my mind and heart, and I was still working and praying through being a less-controlling, kinder version of myself. That in and of itself was like a full-time job. I was also working part-time as director of women's ministries and taking graduate classes, our children played multiple sports, and Chris traveled on business frequently. Time was more precious than oxygen. I had very little margin in my life for anything extra, let alone a troubled, almost-teenaged boy whom we knew almost nothing about except for his egregious background and behaviors. How, why, and where could we add something or someone to our lives?

Despite my rational understanding of these and other legitimate reasons, I could not forget Foley. I could not reconcile a child, through no fault of his own, going through what Foley had in twelve years of life. He and his sister were supposed to be adopted by a foster family, but because of Foley's egregious behavioral and academic struggles, the family only adopted his sister. He had lived as a ward of the state for most of his life. When I was doing more fact-finding about Foley, I went on the website where he and many other children like him were featured. I wondered, *What difference would it make*? I questioned how helping one among thousands of children would matter. What difference would it make to help one child?

When I was driving home one day thinking about that very question, I thought of my own son. I thought about what difference it would make if someone loved him if he were in Foley's situation. I wondered if I would think the same way if I knew it were my son who went to bed in a group home, only received side hugs, and was visited at best for an hour or two by only a few people: caseworkers, the judge who had befriended him, and occasionally the woman who adopted his sister. It was akin to being a prisoner, but he had not done anything wrong. I wondered if I would question what difference it would make if Foley were my son. Very quickly it became clear doing nothing was not an option, so we decided to do something.

To PONDER: When were you afraid to serve or afraid while serving?

• • • •

WHAT SOMETHING LOOKS LIKE

"Religion that God our Father accepts as pure and faultless is this: to look after orphans and widows in their distress and to keep oneself from being polluted by the world." James 1:27

On one of our many fact-finding visits with the state about Foley, the staff told us no one who had ever come into his life had stayed, so in whatever capacity we were going to be involved, they asked us for a *lifetime* commitment. The word "lifetime" scared us more than anything in our journey with Foley, but after more prayer, difficult conversations, meetings with the state, and background checks, we decided what doing *something* would look like.

Although we decided we could not adopt Foley because of the age of our girls (the state also advised against us adopting him for that reason), we decided to mentor him. I was going to tutor him and use my education and experience in behavioral disabilities to help him academically. As a family, we were going to show him, for possibly the first time, a (relatively) normal family. When you are removed from your home by the state before you start kindergarten and you have grown up moving from group home to group home, you do not know what family means or looks like. We hoped perhaps we might be able to help him enough with socialization and academics that he would someday get adopted. Mentoring Foley was something we could do, for a lifetime.

I met Foley on May 22, 2013. I thought I was going to be sick on the twenty-five-minute drive to the residential facility where he lived. I had only seen one picture of him, and it was several years old. With the exception of the redeeming things the judge said about Foley in the article I initially read, I was told mostly about the volatile and difficult things about Foley. I was buzzed into the sunny, well-lit building and given a visitor lanyard. Finally I saw the familiar face of the caseworker I had met through the state; she met me and took me to a room to wait for Foley. When he came in, Foley could not sit still in his seat, maintain eye contact, or stop smiling. He was a happy young man but very distracted and energetic.

The first several times I went to the residential facility after that, I played games with Foley, got to know him, and helped him with his schoolwork. Occasionally I would bring him a shake or coloring book, but usually I just came and we talked and played games. Besides the long commute to the facility, which I did not have time for, every visit was difficult. I did not know what to expect in the forty-five minutes I had alone in the windowless, dark visitors' room where we usually met. Most of the children and teenagers at the facility seemed to have more severe behavioral needs than Foley. Seeing staff struggling with the teenagers and hearing kids yelling, swearing, or worse made it hard to leave Foley. The staff was generally pleasant; however, many seemed like they did not want to be there. To be honest, I did not blame them. It was a depressing and difficult place to be, even for forty-five minutes and even for a former special education teacher.

After a few months, I introduced Foley to each of my kids, and they would color or play games with him. They really enjoyed Foley and found him funny and sweet. Chris came to the facility, too. He interacted with Foley and often commented on his energy level. After several months of getting to know him, we took Foley on his first picnic. He asked me to bring "one of those things with the red squares" for us to sit on, so I did. After we ate our lunch, my son and husband played catch with him.

Eventually we took Foley day camping, where he made his first s'mores and complained vehemently and constantly on a wilderness walk through the woods. Everything was new to Foley. Things my kids took for granted, things like family time, campfires, and getting help tying your shoe from your dad, were things Foley had never known.

We were always cognizant of trying to ensure that Foley understood that we were friends and not family, since we could not adopt him. However, after meeting with him regularly for about six months, he ended up staying overnight at our house. It was Christmas Eve, and I had arranged with the staff at the group home Foley had recently transitioned to that we were going to pick him up and take him to church. When we arrived, however, the man on staff told me Foley would be at the home by himself the next few days. He explained the other seven boys were going to be with family over Christmas. I remember feeling sick and conflicted. I walked back to our car where my family was ready and waiting, and I told my husband Foley was going to be the only child at the group home over Christmas. We agreed that was unacceptable, so Foley packed a bag. We took him to Christmas Eve service and then took him to our home. He slept in our office next to our master bedroom, where I slept with one eye open. The next morning, Foley opened his Christmas gifts along with the rest of our kids and stayed until the following morning.

Foley was happy, naughty, and unpredictable. Once I picked Foley up and he told me with a big smile on his face that he did not want to see us anymore. He was afraid of bugs and the dark. Sometimes when we would take him back to the residential facility at night, he would get very anxious and hide his head in his hoodie, shiver, and whimper because he did not like the dark. He was usually grateful but would pout and be obstinate, too.

On one visit, he got very upset with me for calling him by his full name, which I had done a hundred times. He walked out of the visitors' room, which he was not supposed to do, and an irritated staff person had to escort him to his room. When we would take

Foley to one of the kids' sporting events, we had to stand where we had room so Foley could bounce. He was so happy to be with us (and he knew he would probably get a snack from the concession stand) that he could not contain himself. Foley taught me very quickly that even doing something small is never simple.

Almost every time we saw Foley or did something with him, it was stressful. I did not want to get attached to him and never be able to do more than the small something we were doing. I worried about my children with him, though in hindsight I did not need to. I worried he would want to live with us and could not. When we had Foley stay for Christmas, I bawled and vented angrily to my husband the second night he was with us. Foley inexplicably became upset and began angrily pulling the yarn out of the hat he had proudly worn the night before. He threw a towel and would not talk to any of us and kept fleeing from room to room in our house.

I was exhausted and frustrated. I wanted Christmas to look like it always had with my immediate family. I did not want to spend time dealing with him acting up Christmas Day. I did not want to be tired because I had not slept well with a thirteen-year-old we had met six months before sleeping on my couch. I did not want to deal with the infected toenail he presented to me on Christmas Eve. This was not the Norman Rockwell Christmas I had envisioned.

What did Foley teach me about what something looks like?

Doing something is complicated and scary and did not look anything like what I thought it would. Doing something challenged my beliefs and cost me time and energy I did not think I could spare. Doing something forced me to confront my idols again. It was humbling, frustrating, and left me with more questions than answers. My biggest question and challenge of all in doing something with Foley, however, was not knowing.

I did not know if I "heard from God" when I read that article about Foley. I did not know if I had been delusional, irresponsible, or obedient to the Spirit by pursuing this opportunity to help. I did not know if God brought Foley to us to answer my prayer for a lifestyle of service. I did not know why, why us, or if we did the right thing. I did not know. Even now, five years after reading about Foley and being in his life regularly (and the life of the man who eventually adopted him), I still do not know.

> To Ponder: When was a time you did something that seemed small but turned out to be significant in your life or the life of the person you helped?

• • • •

Hearing From God

"For God does speak – now one way, now another – though man may not perceive it." Job 33:14

Not knowing was the most difficult part of my journey with Foley. It was difficult not just because of the decision and discernment I needed with him, but the trajectory of my life had been based on "hearing from God." When my children were young and I was attending a Mothers of Preschoolers (MOPS) group, I thought I heard the Spirit's whisper, too. As the presenter was sharing, I remember wondering what it must be like to equip and encourage women as a public speaker. I attributed that thought to the Holy Spirit, because public speaking was one of my biggest fears in life.

Soon after starting a MOPS group at our home church, I began speaking more and eventually got calls from other churches asking me to speak as well. I felt God was affirming that I return to teaching but teaching women instead of children. While attending a conference one day, I felt that same Spirit-inspired whisper again while reading James 3:1: "Not many of you should presume to be teachers, my brothers, because you know that we who teach will be judged more strictly." I felt the Lord prompting me to undergird my speaking and teaching ministry by going back to school to learn more about the Bible.

In my everyday life as a wife and mother, I had relied on hearing from the Holy Spirit, too. I often prayed, as Solomon did in 1 Kings 3:9, for God to give me wisdom and discernment before I would discipline my kids or talk to them about a struggle they were having. When I would remember to pray for the Spirit's help, I would respond without defaulting to my usual manipulation and sarcasm tactics. I found I had more patience and responded in a more loving, less controlling way. I was so sure the Spirit was working in me that I taught hundreds of women to pray and ask the Holy Spirit for help in their parenting, too. When in arguments with my husband, I would reluctantly ask God to take my thoughts captive and make them obedient to Christ (2 Corinthians 10:5b).

I saw the Spirit help me there, too, but now I questioned whether I could be obedient if I was unsure of whether or how I had heard God. Had I *ever* heard from the Holy Spirit if I got the

Foley prompting wrong? Although I had previously questioned *what* I heard from God, *why* God took so long to answer, and other questions related to hearing from God, I had never really doubted—once I did hear that it was the Lord speaking and not a bad taco I had eaten the night before.

Until Foley.

My husband prayed about whether we should adopt Foley and heard a resounding "no." A close and dear Christian friend told me maybe I wanted to adopt Foley, so that is what I thought I heard the Spirit say. I did not want anything to do with Foley, which was in part why I thought it was the Lord prompting me, but I did not know. I remember reading Christian books on hearing from the Spirit, asking friends, and looking through my Bible for answers, but I still did not know. I did not know if the Lord had called us to adopt Foley.

The bad news is that I still do not know. I do not know with complete assuredness whether God had called us to adopt Foley or not. The bad news is that I cannot prove how, when, or if we hear from the Holy Spirit. The Holy Spirit is a mystery even though I want Him to be an equation, formula, or other pattern I can replicate when I need answers. But the good news was reading, praying about, and studying the Bible to find out more about the Holy Spirit taught me many things, including perhaps there was a lot I did not need to know.

> To PONDER: When was a time you thought you heard from the Holy Spirit? When was a time you doubted whether you heard from Him?

• • • •

The Great Unknown

"So faith comes from hearing, and through hearing the Word of Christ." Romans 10:17 (ESV)

When I want to hear from God, I want to hear clearly. I want a winged fairy to descend from the sky with a written proclamation, preferably on glowing parchment paper, instructing me exactly what to do and say or how to be obedient. One of the most frustrating things about doing something with Foley was constantly telling God I would do anything He wanted but never hearing clearly as to what that something was. When the winged fairy never showed up, I got frustrated, grew impatient, and turned to Christian friends, pastors, and books to try and discern how to hear God. That made things even worse. It reminded me of when my firstborn suffered from extreme colic. My mother would tell me to put cereal in her bottle, my friend told me to give her formula, and my mother-in-law suggested I try nursing more often. They all loved me and had good intentions, but I did not know who to listen to. I did not know who was right.

Too many of us abstractly believe the Bible is the inerrant, inspired Word of God. Why do I turn to my friends, pastor Matt Chandler, or that book about the Holy Spirit instead of the Bible when I have questions? Because I only believe abstractly that the Bible will help. I also feel I will find the answer more quickly and clearly somewhere else. I am afraid I will miss it or confuse the answer if I read it in the Bible. The ironic part about looking for answers somewhere other than the Bible is that one of the primary ways the Holy Spirit manifests Himself in us and speaks to us is helping us better understand God's Word.[11]

What did the Spirit say to me when I finally turned to the Bible to hear what to do about Foley? When I read Proverbs 24:11-12 (NIV), I felt affirmed that we needed to do something.

"Rescue those being led away to death; hold back those staggering toward slaughter. If you say, 'But we knew nothing about this,' does not he who weighs the heart perceive it? Does not he who guards your life know it? Will he not repay everyone according to what they have done?"

I knew doing nothing was not an option when I read in James 2:15-17, "Suppose a brother or a sister is without clothes and daily food. If one of you says to them, 'Go, I wish you well; keep warm and well fed,' but does nothing about his physical needs, what good is it? In the same way, faith by itself, if it is not accompanied by action, is dead."

Although I had read these passages before, this time I was desperate. The Spirit not only revealed answers to me because I was delving more deeply into Scripture, He also spoke into my situation with Foley because what I was reading was interfacing with real life and a real problem I needed help with. The answers I found did not answer my question specifically, but they refuted clearly that doing nothing was an option. They also affirmed without question that we had to do something.

When we look to the Bible for clarity, answers, and wisdom, the Spirit does not just teach us. He reveals to our hearts and

---

[11] Erickson, 889-90.

minds deeper spiritual truths and understanding of the heart of Christ.[12] When we immerse ourselves more fully in God's Word and see disconnects, feel conviction, and notice life intersecting with what we read, the Spirit takes us deeper. Being in Luke prompted that nagging feeling there was more to successfully parenting my children than giving them every comfort, need, and protection, even though I had orchestrated everything around those ends for fifteen years. It was the Lord who clothed me with the humility to begin seeing what was noble, right, and admirable in my husband after trying for two decades to change. I had walked by the poor and marginalized for forty years until the Spirit began illuminating my heart and mind to His Word and Christ's compassionate, humble, and loving heart in a new and deeper way.

When we look to the Bible, instead of our own conflicted hearts and minds, well-meaning friends, or even pastors who all tell us something different, we also realize the Spirit speaks to us and helps us look more like Christ.[13] Did I hear from God regarding Foley? Did I hear from Him correctly and my husband did not? I may not know the answers to those questions, but I do know this: doing something with and for Foley, in Jesus' name, changed the trajectory of a young man's life. Getting involved in an uncomfortable, inconvenient, and undesirable relationship helped our family learn compassion, generosity, and unconditional love in a way we never had. Following what we thought was the Holy Spirit merely meant doing *something*— something we could agree upon, something that helped someone

---

[12] Ibid., 889.
[13] Ibid., 890.

"Doing nothing is not an option."

in need, and something that taught our family in a tangible way what it looked like to be Jesus' hands and feet.

How do we know if we heard the Spirit when He is not clear, we do not know what to do, and hearing Him leads to more difficulty and work? We keep praying. We check what we believe to be the voice of God against what His Word says. We ask if what we think we hear is helping us grow in love, joy, peace, patience, kindness, goodness, faithfulness, gentleness, and self-control. We talk and pray with the people we do life with who also try to the best of their ability to hear from the Spirit. Then, I believe, we do *something*.

I recently met an orphan girl in China. I could not stop thinking about her, so I asked our friends in China who introduced us to her if we could help her somehow. They said we could not really do anything, and with the language barrier, it has been difficult advocating for her and trying to do something practical to help her. I cannot even send a package or funds to her because I cannot get an address (I do not write, read, or speak Chinese). Do I believe the Spirit called me to her? I do not know. I know my heart is broken for her, however, and doing nothing is not an option.

The only something I can do is pray for her, so I have been. Almost daily I pray for Sunyi. I pray for her like she was my child; often I pray tearfully. I am challenged when I pray, of course. Challenged about what I believe about prayer, what difference it makes, and why I have the constant, nagging feeling there must be something more or better to do than pray. Do

I believe the Spirit called Sunyi to me? I do not know, and I do not need to know. What I need to do is remain prayerful, continue processing all of it in Christian community, and search passionately in God's Word to determine what *something* looks like. Despite my many questions, I am trying to rest in that and trust God with the rest.

To PONDER: What passage of Scripture has God used to help you with a decision, show you His love, or convict you?

••••

Chapter Two:
The Disconnect —
Putting it All Together

Read 2 Timothy 3:14-17

[14] But as for you, continue in what you have learned and have become convinced of, because you know those from whom you learned it, [15] and how from infancy you have known the Holy Scriptures, which are able to make you wise for salvation through faith in Christ Jesus. [16] All Scripture is God-breathed and is useful for teaching, rebuking, correcting and training in righteousness, [17] so that the servant of God may be thoroughly equipped for every good work.

Reflect

2 Timothy 3:16 says, "All Scripture is God-breathed and is useful for teaching, rebuking, correcting and training in righteousness, so that the servant of God may be thoroughly equipped for every good work."

This passage says we hear from the Spirit primarily through the Scripture, and when we hear from Him, we learn. I read and journaled and prayed like never before when I read about Foley. I learned more about what God's Word said in those eight weeks than I had during some of my seminary classes. Paul also tells Timothy we hear from the Spirit when we are reprimanded and corrected, as I found out that fateful Black Friday. However, it was that situation that taught me and allowed me to traverse through conversations with Chris about Foley with self-control, love, and humility. Lastly, we hear from the Spirit when we are trained in righteousness. 1 Corinthians 1:30 and 1 John 2:29 tell us Jesus *is* our righteousness. The Spirit teaches us to look more and more like Jesus in our hearts, homes, and beyond.

Although I cannot say definitively how we hear from the Holy Spirit, the Bible tells us that the Spirit does speak to us (Ezekiel 36:27, John 16:13, Galatians 4:6, 5:18, 1 John 2:27, Luke 12:12, 1 Corinthians 2:12-13), for what purpose He speaks (2 Timothy 3:16, John 14:16-17, 1 Corinthians 12:7), and what we are to do when we hear Him: "so that the man of God may be thoroughly equipped for every good work" (2 Timothy 3:17). There is a mystery to the Holy Spirit, but when we can confirm in Scripture what we think He is telling or calling us to, the important thing is doing something. Doing something reconciled the tension between being obedient to what I sensed the Spirit calling me to do with Foley and my relationship with my husband. Doing something did not look anything like I would have guessed. Doing something may not seem like something, but something, no matter how big or small, is why the Spirit speaks to us.

PRAY

What are you struggling to hear God in right now? Romans 8:26 says, "In the same way, the Spirit helps us in our weakness. We do not know what we ought to pray for, but the Spirit himself intercedes for us with groans that words cannot express." Spend three minutes in uninterrupted prayer asking God to help you with your struggle.

CHAPTER THREE:
LOSING MY RELIGION

"Examine yourselves to see whether you are in the faith; test yourselves." 2 Corinthians 13:5a

My call to the city, difficult as it was at times, was nothing when paralleled to my call to a deeper faith. This five-year call challenged my abstract beliefs so much I almost walked away from a twenty-year relationship with Christ altogether. While going to school, working on marriage and idolatry revelations, and managing all the ins and outs of living my mostly mundane life, I began to have a crisis of faith. I thought I believed God was enough. I would sing in church, "Jesus is All I Need." Abstractly I trusted God no matter what, and I praised Him in the storm.

Until it started raining.

My struggle with doubt started long before Foley, the book of Luke, or Black Friday, and it began with the kind of thing God always uses to work in our lives: the ordinary. My daughter had been complaining for several days about her mouth hurting. When I took her in, she ended up having not one but two abscessed teeth. After a double root canal, she was having such significant pain and swelling we ended up in the emergency room at Children's Hospital. For a week, my daughter writhed

"God uses our lives to WAKE US UP."

in pain, moaning all night. To make matters more chaotic, we had just moved, my older kids' best friends were staying with us because their parents were out of the country, and my husband was out of state on business. After the double root canal, five sleepless nights, and the trip to the ER, where two nurses helped me hold my child down for multiple shots, by the end of the week, we ended up at the oral surgeon for an emergency extraction of both teeth.

God uses our lives to wake us up. He is constantly using things big and small in the secular and commonplace areas of our lives to speak to us. God spoke to Moses while he hung out with sheep in the desert (Exodus 3), He saved Daniel who was merely being obedient at work (Daniel 3), and He taught Martha while she made dinner and cleaned her house (Luke 10:38-42). We want God to meet us in extraordinary and overt ways when we make time for Him to speak, but the reality is that He meets us on a fishing boat (Luke 5:1-11), when playing with our kids (Luke 18:15-17), and when we are climbing trees (Luke 19:1-9). Although I know there are many more egregious, glamorous, or exciting God stories than a root canal, the reality is that God usually speaks to us in the "dailies," as my friend Elaine calls the boring, everyday things that make up most of our lives.

At some point shortly after the root canal, I found myself being annoyed by cliché Christian songs on the radio. I sat in staff meetings at the church where I worked and wondered if the pastors, worship leaders, and others struggled with doubt. I was on a spiritual roller coaster, often plunging into valleys of skepticism and frustration about God, the Bible, and Christianity. Occasionally I would ascend upward and experience peace, be given an answer, or resolve some theological tenet, only to inevitably fall into another pit of despair and angst. I began to wonder if God was good if He allowed suffering great and small, and I wondered if, at the end of the day, being a Christian mattered. Was life any richer, better, or more meaningful following Christ?

The root canal incident came and went. I was still riding the ups and downs of doubt and skepticism about faith, but I was still reading my Bible, praying, and teaching my children about the Lord. We had by this time started mentoring Foley, I was taking classes in seminary, and although my struggle with faith and doubt continued to ebb and flow, I was keeping everything in check.

Until I took my first class on systematic theology.

Learning about predestination in theology class undid something in me. I knew predestination referred to "God's choice of individuals for eternal life or eternal death,"[14] but I thought that meant God knew who was going to choose to believe in Jesus Christ. If God knew who was going to choose Him, He would still know before the creation of the world who would have eternal death or life, but it would be based on "the lostness of the non-elect to their own choice of sin rather than to the active decision of God . . ."[15] The more I studied my textbooks and the Bible, however, the more evidence there was refuting my previous understanding of predestination that God merely

---

[14] Erickson, 921.
[15] Ibid., 931.

knows who will choose Him.[16] I studied everything I could to refute this new information and view of predestination, but eventually I realized I could not, with great certainty or biblical evidence, support what I previously understood predestination to mean. The problem was if it was the "active decision of God" and not a person's choosing that determined who would be saved, it also meant by default that God chose who would be damned.[17]

We can sometimes accept concepts, theology, and the Bible in a story with no names, faces, or feelings. We can more readily accept someone's injustice, suffering, or fate when it does not directly affect us. However, when it is our child, sibling, or spouse, the bias becomes intolerable, or, in my case, minimally irreconcilable. I have a close family member who does not love, believe in, or follow Jesus. I could not understand, reason, or explain how God could be good or loving if He chooses who among His creation would be saved or would suffer. How could I teach women and my own children about an all-loving, all-benevolent God who would choose one of my family members (and others) to be doomed? Not only did that contradict a God who was good, it seemed incredibly unfair.

To Ponder: When have you struggled with doubt? What was the situation surrounding your crisis of faith?

---

[16] Ibid., 936-39.
[17] Ibid., 926-27.

• • • •

THROW ME A BONE

"And the peace of God, which transcends all
understanding, will guard your hearts and your minds in
Christ Jesus." Philippians 4:7

My crisis of faith was indeed a crisis. Everything in my world revolved around my faith in Jesus Christ. I had worked hard to teach our children their entire lives about the importance of a relationship with Him. I had left teaching to pursue my graduate degree in theological studies to undergird my speaking and writing ministry. My faith in a good and fair God was the center and foundation of everything in my life.

Why? It was God and the Bible that had helped me overcome my lifelong battles with fear and anxiety. Nothing I tried helped me overcome panic attacks I had suffered since I was five years old. Nothing until I began studying, praying, and beginning to believe what the Bible said about fear, peace, and God Himself that finally helped me begin to be released from that bondage. Since then, I had poured everything into raising my children, who right, wrong, or indifferent meant everything to me, to believe in this loving, forgiving, and merciful God.

But was He?

The next nine months were grueling. I existed in the dichotomy between all I thought I believed and had designed my life around and this new realization that perhaps God was entirely and inexplicably unfair. When I first struggled with doubt after the root canal debacle, I remember reading the

Psalms and wondering about David's emotional and mental stability. David begins Psalm 13, for example, asking the Lord, "How long O Lord? Will you forget me forever?" but ends the same Psalm, "I will sing to the Lord for he has been good to me." However, when I had my own crisis of faith, David's spiritual and emotional oxymorons began making sense. Opposing thoughts and feelings coexisted in my mind constantly for those nine months. I would oscillate between doubt and faith. I was angry at God but would catch myself praying. I did not understand predestination, but when someone was talking to me about a school shooting, I wanted to tell them about the hope I had in Christ. For almost a year, I was mad, confused, and at times apathetic toward God, yet I did not know how to do life without His Word, prayer, or Him.

Fortunately or unfortunately, I am wired with the innate inability to write or speak about anything I do not resolutely believe. Often, during this season of doubt and confusion, I would learn something or see a glimpse of God I could share with my family or ministry. Although I was honest when teaching at a conference or writing a blog post about my faith struggles, I only did so once I had learned something during my brief stints outside of the pit of doubt and disillusionment with God. Sometimes, however, I had to speak or go to work when I had not learned anything recently or seen God's hand at work. Sometimes I had to lead, teach, or serve but could not, if I could not do so authentically. So often during those nine months, out of desperation, I would simply ask God to throw me a bone.

"I would simply ask God to throw me a bone."

On one such occasion, I was driving to work when I was the director of women's ministries to facilitate an end-of-the-year dialogue with several key leaders. I was still compiling Scripture and researching my Bible and theology books, trying to understand predestination. I was sick to my stomach driving to work, not sure how I was going to pray, let alone get through an entire meeting. I remembered asking the Lord bluntly and angrily to give me *something*. Since I could not fake it but had to get through that meeting, I did the only thing I knew to do even though I was mad at God. I would pray and ask God to throw me a bone. No matter how mad, frustrated, or confused I was during my season of doubt and confusion, the reality was there was something inside me that wanted to stay. I wanted to believe. I wanted God back, but I did not know how to reconcile all I had been learning, and in hindsight, I know that God knew.

When I had to do anything in Jesus' name and I could not rationalize, postulate, or explain what I wanted to believe, He would, in fact, throw me a bone. When I could not manufacture or conjure it up on my own, I would see a glimmer of truth or something in my life that intersected with what I was reading in the Bible. I would hear a whisper that kept me hobbling along. There were glimpses of God, often inexplicable ones, that allowed me to do ministry without lying, compromising, or faking.

For example, just before arriving to work to facilitate that end-of-the-year meeting, the feelings of anxiety, anger, and the dark cloud of doubt and confusion just left. A supernatural spirit of contentment, peace, and assuredness saturated me, and I was able to facilitate out of a spirit of humility, love, and authenticity. There were other "bones," too. Though I was doubting God's goodness during this time, when someone started talking to me about why he left church, I was suddenly overcome with concern and care for him, so much so that I started sharing that I was a Christian and talking with him about why he left the church. When one of my kids was upset with someone bullying them, although part of me wanted to chase the offender down with mama bear fury, the Spirit prompted me to pray with my kids for the bully.

As I have mentioned before, one of my passions for ministry and for this book is to thwart the expectation of an easy, neat, safe, and understandable faith. I have had too many romantic, unrealistic, and unbiblical hopes about what faith in Jesus Christ should look like. I am an American living in the twenty-first century. I do not want nebulous explanations about the supernatural work of the mystery of the Spirit; however, the reality of the Christian walk is that God is God and we are not. We are not always going to get answers we want or believe we need, in part simply because we are human, finite, and not omniscient or omnipresent humans. I am not suggesting we follow God with blind or ignorant faith that does not ever wrestle with doubt or have questions. However, I have learned that sometimes I have to rest in the bigness of the God who made the heavens and the earth.

During my five-year journey questioning and struggling with doubt about faith in Christ, things happened sometimes that were difficult to articulate and explain. That was humbling, but part of what I needed to come to a deeper, more meaningful faith was to learn the humility that comes when I remember I am not God. Part of how I reconciled predestination and fell in love with the Lord again came from simply realizing my own smallness.

> To PONDER: When has the Spirit done something inexplicable in your life?

. . . .

GIVING UP

". . . but the message they heard was of no value to them, because they did not combine it with faith." Hebrews 4:2b

How did I finally reconcile predestination? At a snail's pace, and after a thousand series of boring events. Like almost every lesson, transformation, and journey in my life, there was no sign or epiphany. There was no moment in time where the light bulb went on and I understood predestination, started loving Jesus again, and went on with my life. Instead, there were many little things that happened over a long period of time, little things that slowly forced me to confront abstract beliefs I had about salvation, the Bible, and the cross.

One of the things that led to my reconciliation with predestination and my relationship with the Lord was simply giving up. I had become so hardened, skeptical, and frustrated with trying that my mom encouraged me to stop. My mother's faithfulness and steadfastness in her belief in Christ over the years was one of the reasons I came back to church and eventually to the Lord in my late twenties. She knew how disgruntled I had recently become and told me to quit trying to be a "good"

Christian and to merely enjoy God, look for His goodness, and thank Him when I saw it.

Once I quit trying, over the span of about six months, the abstract concept of salvation I understood on paper and cerebrally started to sink. Christ's death on the cross for my eternal salvation, and for abundant life, now for the first time slowly became a core belief I understood in my heart. Not heart as in emotionally per se, but heart as in a fuller and more whole, a richer and deeper understanding of the free gift of grace Christ afforded me. Jonathon Edwards called this heart understanding "affections." "Affections are, of course, filled with emotions, but they are not identical to them. Affections are the inclination of the whole person when sensing the beauty and excellence toward some object . . . Affections, however, are more enduring and involve both the convictions of the mind and changes in life and action."[18] After twenty years of being a Christian, reading my Bible, praying daily, and even pursuing my degree in theological studies, my doubt, disdain, and inability to reconcile predestination eventually ended in a deeper, richer sense of the "beauty and excellence" of Christ's personal, intimate, and unconditional love for me.

When my mother went home to Japan after many years of living in the United States and becoming a Christian, she tried sharing Christ with her family. They said Christianity sounded nice and they were happy for her, but it sounded too easy and too good to be true. It sounded like a fairy tale they could not believe and, looking back, I do not think I did either.

Most of my Christian life, I said—and abstractly believed—

---

[18] Keller, 160-61.

that serving the poor, volunteering to teach Sunday School, trying to drive the speed limit, not losing my temper, and other "measurable" works did not affect my standing in God's eyes. I knew on a cerebral level that I was justified and had been declared legally forgiven. However, underneath a wishful, cerebral, and abstract understanding of being saved by grace through faith, I was living out of the core and subconscious belief that if I could be holier, act better, and volunteer more, I would be more loved, accepted, and pleasing to God. Although Paul talks in Romans about "the obedience that comes from faith" (1:5), I had reversed the order. My obedience, or lack of it, was the litmus test I used to measure my faith, righteousness, and worth. Therefore, my behavior, words, and service were motivated more by obligation than an overflow of Christ's love for me.

To Ponder: When have you struggled with Christ's offer for eternal life and forgiveness feeling or seeming to be too easy?

• • • •

Yelling at My Kids

"For as high as the heavens are above the earth, so great is his love for those who fear him; as far as the east is from the west, so far has he removed our transgressions from us." Psalm 103:11-12

One of the many things that helped slowly move my abstract, head knowledge of Jesus Christ to a core, heart-knowledge understanding was one morning when I unleashed mom rage at my daughter. I was meeting a new friend who oversaw a large ministry, had a great family, and was adorable inside and out. Without realizing it, I felt an underlying, subconscious need to impress her. Ensuring that my outfit was perfect and my shoes complemented my jewelry were my focus the morning we were meeting, but watching the clock was not. I ended up running grossly behind, and the only person I could blame for my tardiness was my daughter. I ran into the kitchen asking why she was not ready, had not gotten her stuff together the night before, and how could she ever expect to hold down a job someday when she was so unorganized. My rage continued until we were almost to school and I calmed down enough to tell her to have a good day and that I loved her, in case that was not painfully obvious.

Immediately after dropping her off and heading, ironically, to Bible study, I was plagued with guilt. My oldest child at that time was eighteen. How in almost two decades of parenting had I not gotten any better? How, after parenting three children into their teenage years, had I not improved? How could it be, despite graduating from middle school so many years earlier, that I was still so worried and threatened about meeting someone who I thought was better than me in every way? I had also spent the only few minutes I would see Faithe that day yelling at her because of my vanity and pettiness.

I stood in worship before heading into Bible study mouthing words I did not care about or believe. All I could think about while singing "Good, Good Father" was that I was a bad, bad mother. Every song made me feel worse. I felt like a hypocrite standing in church with real Christian women who probably did not blame their kids when they ran late so they could look perfect.

During the last song of worship, however, I finally heard the words I was singing. I do not remember the song, but it was about Christ's forgiveness. It was about the cross and God's grace, and I remember mouthing the words and hearing the Spirit ask me, "Well, which is it?" I was convicted in love by the Holy Spirit about what I really believed. Was I too big a jerk, too bad a mom, and too much a repetitive failure for Christ's love and forgiveness? Was I acting out of the belief Christ's death covered my sinfulness yesterday and today, or had my sin gotten bigger than His power to forgive?

"Was I too big a jerk, too bad a mom, and too much a repetitive failure for Christ's love and forgiveness?"

I realized in that moment that my guilt, sorrow, and shame had overshadowed Christ's death. I had become my own best distraction to the cross. I realized that looking inward at my failures instead of upward to the completeness of Christ's death on the cross had robbed me of worshipping and thanking the God of second chances. In that moment, one of many moments to come, I began to understand Christ's love for me in a deeper, more life-giving way.

How did I traverse the chasm of five years of doubt about God? How did I reconcile predestination? How did I decide I finally, firmly resolved that I was not going to leave Christianity? In short, it was the process of knowing in my heart, not just my mind, the depth of Christ's unconditional love and mercy. It was understanding that I was trying to earn God's approval and love by proving I was a good mom, volunteer, and human being. It was realizing that my behavior, shortcomings, or successes were not how God defined or saw me because of Christ's death on the cross. It was learning that sanctification was only possible because of justification. It was believing in my core that God did not see me without sin because I was good. Christ came because I am a hot mess who will never be wholly and completely morally sanctified in this life, though that is my goal.[19] When Christ's love became more than something I wanted or thought I should believe, the questions surrounding even predestination were overshadowed by my affection for my Father. I began to trust regardless of what I could explain or see that God was in fact incredibly and indescribably good, merciful, and loving.

What has moved many of my once-abstract beliefs to core ones that affect how I live more often? Until we come to the place where we taste the honey we have read about or heard about on Sunday, believed to be sweet, and mentally ascribed to, we will reverse the order of faith and doing. We will find our identity and worth in our obedience or failure to obey. We consciously or subconsciously will continue to act out of the mistruth and abstract belief we are acceptable or unacceptable based on performance. What helped me begin to serve with greater longevity, more godly intent, joy, and impact? By learning and continuing to learn painfully and slowly how to find my worth, identity, and acceptance in the person and work of Jesus Christ.

I soon began to learn, however, that until I could see my own brokenness and need for Christ apart from my works and worth, I would also continue to ignore the poor and homeless. I would continue to be my own best distraction to the cross and

---

[19] Erickson, 986.

continue looking inward instead of upward. I would continue to see the marginalized as service projects, as different and as less than—when, at the foot of the cross, they are just like me.

But did I really believe that?

To PONDER: Pastor Matt Chandler said, "God is not in love with some future version of you. It's not you tomorrow that He loves and delights in. It's not you when you get your act together . . . If you believe that Christ's love for you is a future love for you, then you dismiss the cross of Christ." Do you think Christ loves you as you are? (You. Not your sister, mother, or BFF. You.)

••••

CHAPTER THREE:
LOSING MY RELIGION —
PUTTING IT ALL TOGETHER

READ LUKE 15:11-24

[11] Jesus continued: "There was a man who had two sons. [12] The younger one said to his father, 'Father, give me my share of the estate.' So he divided his property between them.

[13] "Not long after that, the younger son got together all he had, set off for a distant country and there squandered his wealth in wild living. [14] After he had spent everything, there was a severe famine in that whole country, and he began to be in need. [15] So he went and hired himself out to a citizen of that country, who sent him to his fields to feed pigs. [16] He longed to fill his stomach with the pods that the pigs were eating, but no one gave him anything.

[17] "When he came to his senses, he said, 'How many of my father's hired servants have food to spare, and here I am starving to death! [18] I will set out and go back to my father and say to him: "Father, I have sinned against heaven and against you. [19] I am no longer worthy to be called your son; make me like one of your hired servants."' [20] So he got up and went to his father.

"But while he was still a long way off, his father saw him and was filled with compassion for him; he ran to his son, threw his arms around him and kissed him.

[21] "The son said to him, 'Father, I have sinned against heaven and against you. I am no longer worthy to be called your son.'

[22] "But the father said to his servants, 'Quick! Bring the best robe and put it on him. Put a ring on his finger and sandals on

his feet. ²³ Bring the fattened calf and kill it. Let's have a feast and celebrate. ²⁴ For this son of mine was dead and is alive again; he was lost and is found.' So they began to celebrate."

REFLECT

Read Luke 15:20 again. When did the father see his son and was filled with compassion for him? Before or after the son apologized? What is the first word of verse 22?

One of the things that happened to me in the six months I quit trying was hearing and seeing a constant barrage of sermons, devotions, and teachings on the prodigal son in Luke 15. When I finally understood, despite reading and hearing that story so many times, the teaching was about the *father*, it started stirring my affections. The parable is not about the son we identify with. I could relate to the prodigal son when I was in high school and college and the equally broken, unworthy older son I morphed into in my late twenties and beyond. The story is about the extravagant, difficult-to-understand, and unconditional love of the father. Reconciling predestination is not about theological tenets, grandiose and complicated explanations, and compiling and comparing Scripture. Reconciling predestination; being a better wife, mother, and human being; and truly helping others is all about understanding in our soul the depth of the Father's love for us.

PRAY

Read Luke 15:11-24 again, but before you do, pray for one minute and ask God to speak to you as you read. Ask Him to show you the depth of His love for you in a new way.

CHAPTER FOUR:
THE COST OF A FRAPPE

"Why do you call me, 'Lord, Lord'
and do not do what I say?" Luke 6:46

Having come to a richer, fuller heart knowledge and embodiment of Christ's grace by His death and resurrection, I continued to learn. Things like yelling at my daughter before Bible study continued to happen, which reaffirmed and reminded me that God did not like me more or think I was better when I did "well." Nor did He shake His head at me when I failed. I began slowly to see His goodness, be more grateful for the daily mercies His death afforded me, and I began taking my eyes off myself more often. I began to realize that when I spent less time feeling guilty and "less than" for my daily and hourly failures, my mind and heart became more available to see others. I slowly began to look more like the wife, mom, and Christ-follower I wanted to be. When I failed, I began to give myself grace more than condemnation and in doing so began experiencing more joy, gratitude, and freedom.

However, when we have a slow journey that leads to a deeper understanding of the cross or a rare one-time epiphany that teaches something new about God or our faith, we are not fixed. Although

I had learned so much, I was still in the process of believing God's love at a core level. I would find myself still gravitating back to my desire to be efficient and improved. I would grow frustrated moving two steps forward then three steps back in being a godlier wife. I understand God is conforming me to Christ's image, but I tire of failing and hurting those I love most along the way. How do we live in the reality of our shortcomings and failures, yet fully covered by and immersed in the love and forgiveness of Christ?

In John 21, Jesus reinstates Peter over a fish breakfast on the beach. Peter was among the three of Jesus' closest disciples who adamantly said he could never forsake Christ, but did. Three times, in fact (Mark 14:72). Peter was not lying when he told Jesus he would not deny Him. He abstractly believed what he said. Like us, Peter desperately wanted to do the right thing and thought he could. Like us, Peter failed and did not fail once, but repeatedly. What is Jesus' response to Peter and to us when we fail repeatedly?

Jesus' first response is to help us differentiate between core and abstract beliefs. He asks Peter something three times. Repetition in the Bible and in life are always worth paying attention to. Three times Jesus asks Peter if he loves Him, and after each of Peter's responses, Jesus tells Peter to do something. N.T. Wright says, "The most remarkable thing about it is that, by way of forgiveness, Jesus gives Peter a job to do."[20] Jesus asks Peter three times to remind Peter not of the three times he betrayed Jesus but of Christ's complete forgiveness because of the cross. Why does Peter need to be reminded? The same reason we do: "There is nothing officially 'on the record against us.' But there may still be plenty in our memories and imaginations:

---

[20] Wright, 162.

old failings, old sores, old wounds. Like a computer with faulty virus-ridden software on the hard disk, we need to have it dealt with before we can operate to maximum efficiency once more."[21]

How do we repeatedly fail as Christ followers but still live, love, and serve like Him? We repeatedly confess and convince ourselves, like Peter, of our love for Jesus and His love for us. Then we get to work. "If you are going to do any single solitary thing as a follower and servant of Jesus, that is what it's built on. Somewhere, deep down inside, there is a love for Jesus, and though (goodness knows) you've let Him down enough times, He wants to find that love, to give you a chance to express it, to heal the hurts and failures of the past, and give you new work to do."[22] As Oswald Chambers says, "Let the past sleep, but let it sleep on the bosom of Christ, and go out into the irresistible future with Him."[23]

One of my mentors, Mary Beth, always says that God loves us too much to leave us where we are. When God in His love convicts us, it is always to remind us of His deep, undying, unfathomable love for us. But it does not stop there. His love is meant to move us. His love is meant to fill us up to overflowing. His love is meant to help us ". . . arise and go to the next thing."[24] Although God had revealed so much to me about the disconnect between my educational, financial, and other areas of surplus and the poor in spirit, resources, and education around me, there was so much more He still wanted to show me because of His great love for me and the people around me.

---

[21] Ibid., 164.
[22] Ibid., 165.
[23] Chambers, Feb 18th.
[24] Chambers, Feb. 18th.

> To Ponder: Recall a time you failed, hurt someone, or let them down more than once that still bothers you when you think about it. Based on Scripture, what do you think God would say to you about this?

· · · ·

Walking by the Homeless

"But he wanted to justify himself, so he asked Jesus, 'And who is my neighbor?'" Luke 10:29

Around the time of my new and greater understanding of the depth of the cross and Christ's love for me, we went to visit my brother in Indianapolis. Some of my family decided to climb a tower in the city's center, but my sister-in-law had wisely counseled us to avoid entering the hot, odiferous space leading to an even hotter more odiferous space at the tower's lookout. So my three kids and I headed to Starbucks to enjoy a frappe and the air conditioning. En route, however, a homeless man stopped us.

I encounter homeless people almost everywhere I travel: in Dallas, New York, Florida, and closer to home in Milwaukee and Chicago. I feel bad when I do, but if I am honest, that is all I have done. I have wondered if giving them money is helping if they use the money for alcohol or drugs. I have also read about professional beggars who have made lucrative careers by pretending they are homeless. My husband had just shown me an article about a business owner in Milwaukee who wanted to employ the homeless, but he had been unable to retain workers.

Due to PTSD from abuse and neglect, many do not have the emotional ability or capacity to get a job or keep one. Partly for these reasons, partly because there are so many homeless people, partly because I do not know what to do, I always do the same thing. I look down and walk by.

Until Indy.

The homeless man started talking to my son, and although we have embarrassingly modeled how to walk by the homeless, my son stopped, and for the first time in a long time, I was forced to look in the eyes of a homeless man—glassy, tired, and desperate eyes. He told us not to be afraid because he just wanted money for french fries. My son asked if I had any change, so I gave the man a dollar. When we walked away, my younger daughter said, "God bless you" to the grateful man, and we went into Starbucks to order twenty-five dollars' worth of *coffee*.

After our visit to Indiana, we went back home. We went back to work, laundry, and everyday life, but God would not let me forget the man I now called, "Indy." God would not let me forget those eyes and my pathetic and callous response. It bothered me I gave him a dollar, but my lack of pity and compassion bothered me more.

"If anyone has material possessions and sees his brother in need but has no pity on him, how can the love of God be in him? Dear children, let us not love with words or tongue but with actions and in truth" (1 John 3:17-18).

I saw someone in need and had no pity. I had closed my heart to a harmless, genuine human being loved by God and created in His image. I had also modeled a closed heart to my children, the same children I had worked so diligently to take to church and to teach and share Christ with. Although one of my justifications for walking by the homeless has been keeping myself and my family safe, it was obvious almost immediately Indy was harmless, homeless, and hurting, but all I wanted to do was get away from him. Ironically, Indy had later wandered into the same Starbucks where we were, and I watched him from a distance, greatly convicted and extremely conflicted. As I watched him look into the trashcans and along window sills, I could not take my eyes off him. He did not just follow us into the coffee shop, however. He followed me around for days, weeks, and months in my heart and in my mind.

To PONDER: Think of a time you encountered a beggar or homeless person and how you responded.

• • • •

NOW WHAT?

"Suppose one of you wants to build a tower. Will he not first sit down and estimate the cost to see if he has enough money to complete it?" Luke 14:28

I did not know what to do with Indy, but unlike my encounter with Foley, I had since had breakfast on the beach with Jesus. I did not resist, stress, and perseverate over what do to, how to do it, and all the what-ifs. Like Peter, I knew more deeply of Christ's love and sacrifice despite my failings. Like Peter, I was falling in love more intimately and personally with Jesus. My motivation to help Foley started as obligation. My motivation to do something with Indy was motivated out of an overflow of gratitude for Christ's love. Service motivated out of obligation is laden with fear to protect, control, and solve situations, people, and outcomes. It is usually self-centered, stressful, and burdensome. Service motivated out of an overflowing of Christ's love and mercy, however, looks more peace-filled, joyful, and thankful.

Although my unrest with Indy was different than it was with Foley, I still was not sure what I was supposed to do. So I started to pray and tried hearing God by immersing myself in His Word. After a few weeks of trying to listen to what I should do, I remembered Ashley. Ashley was a woman I had met in seminary through a mutual friend. She was the director of a place called Hope Street in the inner city of Milwaukee. I was not sure what Hope Street was, what Ashley did, or why I thought of her, but after more prayer and confirmation from Scripture, I decided to do something.

I called Ashley, and we met for coffee. I told her my embarrassing story about Indy. I told her I was not sure why I was meeting with her, but I felt compelled to tell her what had happened. When she started getting teary, I thought I had hurt her feelings or she was emotional because I was so heartless toward the homeless she loved and served. Ashley, however, explained that about six months before we met, she felt the Lord prompting her to pray for me. Around that time, she had invited me and Chris to a fundraiser event for Hope Street, but we could not attend. She did not know why or what she was supposed to pray for me, but she obediently did. When we were meeting about Indy, she started to understand why God had called her to pray for me. She asked me to join the Hope Street board of directors.

I did not say yes to Ashley right away. I wanted to be sure this was where the Lord wanted me. I had recently stepped off another two-year board position I thought I was supposed to accept. One of my closest friends counseled me to accept that position, and I did not see any red flags; however in hindsight, I am not sure I had waited on the Lord for an answer. The position turned into an obligation I dreaded, because although it was a wonderful Christian organization, my heart was not fully vested in the mission of the organization. It was not where I was supposed to be, and it was not a position where I could utilize my writing, speaking, and photography gifts.

I had also been convicted for a few years prior to this about what the Bible had to say about commitment. 2 Corinthians 8:11 says, "Now finish the work, so that your eager willingness to do it may be matched by your completion of it . . ." Psalm 15:4 talks about keeping an oath even when it hurts. There are a plethora of opportunities to help, serve, and volunteer in wonderful and worthwhile ways, but too often I have made decisions to do too many good things or even a few good things without patiently praying or giving any consideration to God's view of making and following through on commitment.

When I contemplated and prayed about the Hope Street position, I was also once again challenged by my idols. Although God has brought me a long way in surrendering my calendar and children to Him, it is still a difficult choice. Prayerfully determining on any given day if I am to serve my family, serve at Hope Street, or tend to my own soul takes time, intentionality, and discernment. Realizing efficiency was an idol did not make waiting, taking time to pray earnestly, and listening any easier.

Being with God instead of doing for Him is hard for some of us.

However, the stakes were high. I needed to pray about whether I could miss a basketball game or two to attend a fundraiser or serve in the city. I needed time to see how deeply I was willing to commit to a lifestyle of service and forgo the things in which I found great pleasure and fulfillment.

While I prayed about Hope Street, I also got to work investigating. I learned that Hope Street was a "Greenhouse for People" that provided housing for formerly broken men, women, and children who could live safely in community and get back on their feet. I went to a prayer meeting at Hope Street and met residents, some of whom were former addicts, inmates, or homeless men, women, and children. I brought my kids to Hope Street and cleaned one of the apartments that had been recently vacated. I attended a long and boring city hall meeting about zoning for a new building Hope Street was in the process of purchasing to expand its ministry. I went to another meeting downtown and photographed the signing of the purchase.

When I would drive to the inner city or downtown, someone always honked at me, and do not get me started on trying to find parking. When I went to the zoning meeting, a construction worker shouted angrily at me for walking under some scaffolding I did not see. Cleaning the third-floor apartment at Hope Street was gross and hot, and I did not appreciate finding a dead mouse on the floor. I was worried about my car getting broken into when I was there, and I did not (and still do not) find the forty-minute commute into the inner city efficient or particularly desirable, but as Jill Briscoe says, "sometimes loving others is just doing the obvious." The more I volunteered at Hope Street, met the residents, and took my family to serve, the more the obvious became obvious. I said yes to the board position and began doing something, in Indy's honor and in Jesus' name.

To PONDER: Think about a time you did something big, small, or somewhere in between, simply out of obedience to a prompting you felt in your heart?

• • • •
DOES THAT HELP?

"Is it not to share your food with the hungry and to
provide the poor wanderer with shelter – when you see
the naked, to clothe him, and not to turn away from your
own flesh and blood?" Isaiah 58:7

One of the many things I am learning since serving at Hope Street is my convoluted definition and understanding of helping. When time and efficiency were my primary and unidentified idols, I helped by making monetary donations because I could make more money but not more time. If I could not attend a fundraiser because I was going to another of my kids' sporting events, I would donate a raffle item. I have given spare change to the homeless, wrapped presents at an inner-city community center, and helped with crafts at a Christmas party for the children of formerly incarcerated men, but I have started to question if I ever really helped at all.

I have learned at Hope Street the things I thought might help someone are often not helpful. Giving money can be a wonderful

> "I have found one of the best ways I can love the members at Hope Street is to ask their story."

way to help the poor, but it can also be nothing more than helping ease my own conscience. Handouts that contribute to an individual's dependence on handouts rather than helping them learn to become independent, if they are able, is not helpful either. Sometimes children whose parents are found using drugs or alcohol must immediately move out of Hope Street. I used to struggle with that because it seemed harsh and merciless. I now realize enabling the use of vices that lead to dysfunction, pain, and patterns of abuse is much harsher and more merciless.

I am also learning what is helpful. Father Greg Boyle, who began and works at Homeboy Industries, a gang intervention program in Los Angeles, says, "The principal suffering of the poor is shame and disgrace."[25] I have found one of the best ways I can love the members at Hope Street is to ask their story. A member usually lights up when I ask them about themselves or how they found out about Hope Street. When I realized Indy was sober, clean, and coherent, I could have, and wished I had, asked him his story. There is something beautiful and therapeutic when any of us shares our story—the sources of our joys and sorrows, the places of our brokenness, and what makes us who we are.

When I was in Shanghai recently, a woman came by, pushing her son in a wheelchair and begging for money. I gave her some

---

[25] Boyle, 52.

loose change, and before Foley and Indy, that would have been all I did. This time I bent over and said hello to the young man in Chinese. The mother and I smiled at each other, one loving mother to another. The more we seek God in doing something for those in need, the more we begin to identify with them. We begin to see that healing and problem-solving happen best in community and relationships. When we do something in Jesus' name, we begin to see our common humanity. We see helping is not just about giving money but also about the heart behind the giving. We begin to learn how powerful eye contact, a smile, or a hug can really be.

To PONDER: When was the last time you intentionally looked someone in the eye (besides a friend or family member)?

• • • •

Chapter Four:
The Cost of a Frappe —
Putting It All Together

READ MATTHEW 9:1-13

Jesus stepped into a boat, crossed over and came to his own town. ² Some men brought to him a paralyzed man, lying on a mat. When Jesus saw their faith, he said to the man, "Take heart, son; your sins are forgiven."

³ At this, some of the teachers of the law said to themselves, "This fellow is blaspheming!"

⁴ Knowing their thoughts, Jesus said, "Why do you entertain evil thoughts in your hearts? ⁵ Which is easier: to say, 'Your sins are forgiven,' or to say, 'Get up and walk'? ⁶ But I want you to know that the Son of Man has authority on earth to forgive sins." So he said to the paralyzed man, "Get up, take your mat and go home." ⁷ Then the man got up and went home. ⁸ When the crowd saw this, they were filled with awe; and they praised God, who had given such authority to man.

⁹ As Jesus went on from there, he saw a man named Matthew sitting at the tax collector's booth. "Follow me," he told him, and Matthew got up and followed him.

¹⁰ While Jesus was having dinner at Matthew's house, many tax collectors and sinners came and ate with him and his disciples. ¹¹ When the Pharisees saw this, they asked his disciples, "Why does your teacher eat with tax collectors and sinners?"

¹² On hearing this, Jesus said, "It is not the healthy who need a doctor, but the sick. ¹³ But go and learn what this means: 'I desire

mercy, not sacrifice.' For I have not come to call the righteous, but sinners."

REFLECT

I have often wondered if I were the paralytic, would I have been somewhat disappointed by how Jesus initially helped me? I look for the immediate fix, quick solution, and temporal comfort. Jesus says in this passage, "I desire mercy, not sacrifice" (9:13). I identify with giving sacrifice. It is measurable, visible, and tangible. Mercy is sometimes manifested in something we can see, but it is predominantly and always foremost a heart issue.

PRAY

Pause for a second. Turn off your mind. Don't think about getting to the end of the book or those dishes in the sink. Pause and take a deep breath. Take one minute to pray about which you would have wanted if you were the paralytic, to be healed or forgiven. Do not pray what you think you should pray, but work through honestly and tell God the why of your answer. Then take thirty seconds (it will seem long) to be still. Perhaps you will hear the Lord. Perhaps you will hear crickets. I am terrible at listening to my spouse, to friends, and to God, but I am practicing. That is the only way we will learn to listen.

> *I desire mercy,*
> *not sacrifice.*
>
> MATTHEW 9:13

CHAPTER FIVE:
WHAT THE
HUMANS TEACH US

"Can a mother forget the baby at her breast and have no compassion on the child she has borne? Though she may forget, I will not forget you! See, I have engraved you on the palms of my hands; your walls are ever before me."
Isaiah 49:15-16

How did I go from ignoring the homeless to identifying with them? When we do something in Jesus' name and come alongside people, we have already established that it can be uncomfortable. When we eat with, walk beside, and talk to people who are different than us and broken, it is uncomfortable. It is uncomfortable mostly because we are forced to see our own brokenness. The Humans, as my friend calls people, are messy, complicated, and difficult. I am messy, complicated, and difficult. The more I went to Hope Street and continued being involved with Foley, the more I was challenged and changed. I began to see I had a tainted view of the worth and value of The Humans: people in the city, the suburbs where I lived, and, yet again, The Human looking back at me the mirror.

I recently began interviewing several members (residents)

of Hope Street for our annual fundraiser. I was chronicling their lives, struggles, and what brought them to Hope Street. Our fundraiser theme was "Known," and I was excited to know our members better. I was exuberant to hear and write their stories, and the members were excited to share their journey. I could not wait to get started.

Until we got started.

The stories of the men and women who come to a place like Hope Street are difficult. They were particularly difficult because as I was becoming aware of my own inability or unwillingness to see everyone as equally worthy, broken, and loved, I thought the interviews would help change that. Foley and Indy were the catalysts the Spirit used to begin moving the abstract belief everyone is created in the image of God to a core belief. I thought the member interviews would help solidify and illustrate God's image in all of us and how great His love is for each of us. In all honesty, the interviews seemed instead to prove the opposite.

Quita's mother sold, used, and abused drugs and had moved their family into a drug house when Quita was a teenager. Men sexually abused Quita and her sisters until Quita begged her mother to take her sisters somewhere safe. Quita, abandoned and alone, began living the only life she had known, a life of prostitution and drug abuse. She repeatedly entered into cycles of drug and alcohol abuse, abusive and dysfunctional relationships, and physical and financial health problems. Quita had forgiven her mother, who had passed away the year before our interview, because "it was all she knew." This was Quita's second time at Hope Street, and at the time of our interview, she had been sober almost a year.

Jerri's father began giving her alcohol when she was seven years old so he could sexually abuse her more easily. Her mother knew about it but denied much of the abuse. Jerri grew up an alcoholic, and until she came to Hope Street seven years ago, she had only known sobriety during her stints inside of jail, in treatment facilities, or in a hospital. Jerri was once in a hospital so long she was unable to attend her daughter's funeral. Jerri was driving drunk when she was involved in an accident that took her ten-year-old daughter's life.

I interviewed Reggie, too. His story was very different than Jerri and Quita's in that he came from a loving home. Growing up, he was never in need physically or financially. Reggie was a gifted athlete and excellent student. Although hopes of a basketball scholarship ended after a difficult and pressure-filled game his senior year, Reggie was awarded an engineering scholarship at the University of Tennessee. However, Reggie had been the target of bullying and teasing because of a life-long speech impediment, so he struggled with confidence. In college, Reggie began partying, was "irresponsible," and eventually dropped out of school. He found himself in a cycle of finding a good job, using his paychecks to buy drugs and alcohol, losing said job, hitting bottom, getting clean, and starting the cycle over again. He had, like Quita, been to Hope Street before and been clean before, but returned to his lifestyle of drug abuse and dysfunctional relationships. At the time of our interview, Reggie had been clean the longest he had ever been (and at the publication of this book, he will have celebrated a year of sobriety).

Although I do not doubt God's goodness, love, or involvement in people's lives abstractly, I struggled with these stories. Although I could empathize with the cycle of behaviors and abuse Jerri and Quita learned from their parents, there were things I could not understand. Where is God's image in the evils done to Jerri and Quita? Where is the law written on the hearts of people who can abuse their own children? Although I could relate to Reggie's confidence struggles, his partying days in college, and regrets from those choices, I was saddened by the continuation and escalation of those choices and his ensuing addiction when he had been so loved and gifted.

In seminary, sometimes studying what seemed to be so painfully obvious was . . . painful. I would skim over topics such as humanity and the image of God in man because they seemed so clear and basic, "So God created man in his own image, in the image of God he created him . . ." (Genesis 1:27a). Got it. Period. End of story. An image of humanity apart from *everyone* being made in God's image seemed to be the image only the cold, heartless, and less thought-filled could conjure up. As I read my Christian theology text, I dismissed the world's view of people as machines having ". . . value as long as they are useful."[26] I passed over ridiculous tenets that viewed people as social beings or pawns of the universe, victims of their fate by a world indifferent to their well-being or worse, that their image was that of sexual machines motivated only by an innate excesses of desires.[27]

However, after Foley, Indy, Quita, Jerri, and Reggie, I realized I had, almost my entire life, subconsciously viewed people as having value only if they were useful. I now began seeing people

---

[26] Erickson, 487.
[27] Ibid., 488-92.

like Jerri as victims of a world indifferent to her well-being instead of seeing her first, apart from her story, as made in the image of God. I resonated with Quita's story and realized that I do see people sometimes as sexual machines I believe to be hopeless, worthless, and useless. Although my own experience was less egregious than Quita's story, I could relate and empathize with the sexual abuse of her past. I had been a victim of sexual assault as a child myself. Although it did not happen repeatedly or in the difficult context and dysfunction Quita had endured, in hindsight, perhaps my abuse has, at times, tainted my perception of men and impacted my core beliefs about them. I have failed to see everyone made in God's image, and I have prematurely assigned motives based on my perception and fears.

The core belief that often prevents us from doing something is believing that "something" is insignificant. Doing something sounds easy, trite, and simple, but I am learning it is far from any of those things. *Something* among many things teaches, challenges, and exposes. *Something* allows the ugly, dark core beliefs to come to the surface—core beliefs that lie, usually subliminally, in our hearts and minds and impact how we see and treat people and places that make us uncomfortable. Getting involved with Foley, being challenged by Indy, and learning the stories of the members at Hope Street is exposing my biased and blind heart. I am realizing I do not see God's image in people because sometimes I am too afraid to look. I am learning when the

> "The core belief that often prevents us from doing something is believing that 'something' is insignificant."

image of God seems nearly impossible to see in people, I do not have the authority to assign them an image other than what the Bible says, the Bible that I profess is true and inerrant.

I am learning I sometimes operate out of the core belief the undeserved are, in fact, undeserved.

When we operate out of abstract beliefs and do not realize it, we can rationalize what is embarrassing to verbalize. We live believing we love others in Jesus' name and see them made in God's image when, in fact, we do not. When we do not challenge whether our beliefs are just that or ones we live and act out of, we live in the most dangerous way possible.

> To Ponder: Think about a time you saw the news or read a paper or met someone whose life or story shocked, appalled, or broke you.

. . . .

What Real Wealth Looks Like

"One of them, when he saw he was healed, came back, praising God in a loud voice. He threw himself at Jesus' feet and thanked him – and he was a Samaritan."
Luke 17:15-16

One of my first mornings at Hope Street, I met Charles Wiggins. Mr. Wiggins is a soft-spoken, seventy-year-old, dapper and handsome African-American man whose voice I could listen to for hours. I enjoy hearing him read a devotional or share a story when he facilitates Hope Street's weekly prayer meeting.

When Charles speaks, everyone within earshot gets quiet and wants to listen. He has a smooth yet intentional way of speaking that is intriguing and almost alluring. As interesting and inviting as it is, however, it is also daunting. Daunting because I struggle with any speed but fast. I am an efficiency person who walks, talks, and drives quickly. Charles understands, however, what I do not. You cannot be intentional and rushed simultaneously. He knows processing well cannot be done quickly. Doing something by attending prayer meetings forced me to do something I want abstractly but do not practice. Charles taught me to be still. There was something else Charles taught me during prayer that I wanted and needed but rarely practiced, as well:

Gratitude.

The first time I attended prayer at Hope Street, while still discerning what my involvement with the homeless was going to be, Charles read from an *Our Daily Bread* devotional. He started to pray and began with thanking God for a tree. He prayed for several minutes, slowly, about a tree in the small courtyard outside Hope Street. The small brick patio was walled in between Hope Street, a condemned brick building next door, and a fenced-off alley, and apparently there was a tree there. Efficiency people like myself do not pay attention to trees, birds, or anything else unless they lend to a purpose or end goal.

But Charles did.

He prayed as if he were standing in front of that tiny tree, head tipped back slightly so he could focus and survey every branch and leaf. I pictured him nodding with approval as he thanked God not only for the tree but for the new life that was blooming in the tiny leaves sprouting from it. With thoughtful pauses and reflection, he thanked God for providing the seasons, for the warmth of the sun, and for the springtime rains we recently had. He thanked God for His goodness in all things, even providing everything needed so a tree in the courtyard could bloom.

For a very long time, Charles thanked God for a tree.

I am not sure how long Charles prayed for the tree. I do not remember, because while he prayed, I sat in the basement of Hope Street fighting back tears. I was not, at one of my first visits to the Greenhouse for People, going to be seen sobbing over a tree.

Obviously it was not foliage that made me emotional. It was the fact that a tree exposed my lack and my brokenness. The tree in its simplicity—and Charles in his willingness to notice and give thanks for such a small and seemingly insignificant thing—spoke to me loudly and with great, loving conviction. I had so much to be thankful for by worldly standards. I had more financial, possibly educational, and other resources than Charles had or perhaps would have, and yet his thanksgiving for a tree revealed to me my poverty and his wealth. Charles' unknowing and unintentional lesson to me about gratitude that day became a pattern with The Humans at Hope Street almost every time I visited, particularly at the weekly prayer meeting.

To PONDER: Think about the last time you thanked God deeply and intentionally for something He did, a prayer He answered, a relationship or individual in your life, or simply for who He is.

••••

THE RICH HUMANS

"My brothers, as believers in our glorious Lord Jesus
Christ, don't show favoritism." James 2:1

Hope Street is located on 26th Street and Capitol Drive in Milwaukee. Capitol Drive is a main street connecting Lake Michigan on the east side of Milwaukee to the western suburban outskirts where I live, about forty minutes from Hope Street. The difference between the houses, people, and shops from the "good" side of Capitol Drive to the other side is substantial, and so is the transformation that happens in me almost every time I commute to and from Hope Street.

No matter how rushed, irritated, or entitled I was arriving to Hope Street, I seemed to leave more thankful, humbled, and peace-filled after interacting with people like Charles. However, as I would head home down Capitol and the topography morphed, I did, too. I found myself becoming increasingly irritated at big houses, perfectly groomed lots, and expensive cars. I saw what real gratitude and joy looked like among the marginalized, yet those of us who seem to have everything are divorcing at a higher rate, are in greater debt than ever, and are often unhappy, unhealthy, and selfish.

Despite living, loving, and doing life among The Well-to-Do Humans, I began to subconsciously judge people I socialized, carpooled, and worshipped with. Off the radar of my own awareness, I began to think I was better than my suburban neighbors and even my Christian brothers and sisters because I was doing *something*. My something was not big, life-changing, or grandiose, but the problem with The Humans is we can get very important, and arrogant, quickly and subconsciously. We can look down on people for having money as we drive our new car to our large home on our acre lot. I had let pride seep in and looked down my nose at people just like me. I had become what John Ortberg warns we are always vulnerable of becoming: "One of the hardest things in the world is to stop being the prodigal son without turning into the elder brother."[28]

When I would drive in either direction down Capitol, I fixated on what I perceived were problems outside my car windows. People with too much or not enough. Buildings that were beautiful or had bars. I saw problems with both the poor in possession or the wealthy I had deemed poor in spirit. Then I realized once again the greater problem was not outside my car window but inside me. As with everything in the Kingdom of God, the issue is not about money, education, or religiosity. Jesus, after all, loved the rich young ruler (Luke 18:18-22, Mark 10:21) and cared deeply for Zacchaeus (Luke 19:1-10) as much as He loved and cared for the poor (Luke 6:20, 14:13). The issue is always my heart. The issue is always whether we see the merciful, benevolent, and loving image of God in the poor and the wealthy, the well-educated, and the high school dropout, and, most importantly, in ourselves.

I am learning as I do my little something with The Humans in my little sphere of life and influence, seeing the image and enough-ness of God in me impacts everything else. Until God moves me to the core belief that His forgiveness, love, and grace

[28] Ortberg, 113.

because of Christ's death on the cross is enough where I fail, when I burn dinner and yell at my kids, I will be unable to see Him in others. Until I operate more often out of the grace and love that is given me by Christ despite my failures and inadequacies, I will also be unable to extend to others the grace and second chances I refuse to accept from Christ. What I am learning from The Humans is that I view and treat others how I view and treat myself. God is bringing me to a place where my heart is beginning to believe He is enough so I do not have to be. I will never be enough, and neither will anyone else. In that place of humility and gratitude, I can better love the poor and the rich, the deserving and seemingly undeserving, and everyone else Christ gave His life for.

To PONDER: When did someone in your everyday coming and going upset you? What did they do, and what was your reaction?

. . . .

I AM STILL AFRAID

". . . though he was chained hand and foot and kept under guard, he had broken his chains and had been driven by the demon into solitary places." Luke 8:29b

A few weeks ago, I was at Hope Street with my youngest daughter taking some photographs. Just before I was about to use my key to enter the building, a glassy-eyed, disheveled man was standing at the door. I could not let him in since he did not live at Hope Street. I asked him if he wanted to go to the employment ministry adjacent to Hope Street where people can get help filling out applications and looking for jobs, but the man would not answer or look at me. He also would not leave, so Faithe and I could not go in. A man from the employment service came out of the entrance and asked the man if he needed help. The man would not speak to him either. One of the Hope Street staff members then came out to try and speak with the man, but to no avail. Eventually the man went into the employment office but within minutes came rushing back out of the building. He never spoke a word but walked over to the curb by the gas station across the street and just stared into the distance.

My daughter later summed up what we were both thinking, "Well, that was scary."

What else am I learning about The Humans and myself as I walk by the homeless? I am still afraid sometimes. I carry pepper spray on my keychain. I lock my doors when I get to the place on Capitol Drive where there are bars on the windows of businesses. Sometimes I abstractly believe everyone is made in the image of God, but on a core level, I also struggle knowing how to interact with people I am sometimes afraid of. I am uncomfortable when children run out to my car at a particularly large and busy intersection near Hope Street, trying to sell me things when I am stopped at a red light. I was afraid when I photographed Foley's football game last fall and high school students around me were pushing each other and using the "n" word. I was uncomfortable driving past a couple with a small baby holding a sign asking for money not far from my suburban home.

What I am learning about The Humans and being uncomfortable is that there are no easy answers or responses.

Doing something in Jesus' name is not neat, defined, or easy. Love never is. Relationships never are. However, as I learn more about the image of God in everyone, including the despondent man outside Hope Street and kids shoving other kids a foot away from me, I am challenged to grow in not only what I believe about The Humans, but what I believe about myself and God.

When my daughter and I left Hope Street, we prayed together for the man who we were afraid of, but even in prayer, I am continually stretched. Is prayer a last resort? An excuse to do nothing else? Do I pray to make myself feel better that I did something, or do I really believe prayer "changes things," as the saying goes. Do I believe prayer is the most powerful, effective thing I can do sometimes and that prayer matters for me and for the recipient of my prayers? Even if I do believe that, is it enough? The Humans remind me once again that God does not compartmentalize faith and life. He does not allow us to grow in our knowledge of Him without giving us the opportunity to be uncomfortable with what He looks like in our everyday coming and going.

To Ponder: What is your biggest fear when you are faced with someone who is homeless or approaches you in the city? What goes through your mind?

....

CHAPTER FIVE:
WHAT THE HUMANS TEACH US
— PUTTING IT ALL TOGETHER

READ LUKE 10:25-37

25 On one occasion an expert in the law stood up to test Jesus. "Teacher," he asked, "what must I do to inherit eternal life?"

26 "What is written in the Law?" he replied. "How do you read it?"

27 He answered, "'Love the Lord your God with all your heart and with all your soul and with all your strength and with all your mind'; and, 'Love your neighbor as yourself.'"

28 "You have answered correctly," Jesus replied. "Do this and you will live."

29 But he wanted to justify himself, so he asked Jesus, "And who is my neighbor?"

30 In reply Jesus said: "A man was going down from Jerusalem to Jericho, when he was attacked by robbers. They stripped him of his clothes, beat him and went away, leaving him half dead. 31 A priest happened to be going down the same road, and when he saw the man, he passed by on the other side. 32 So too, a Levite, when he came to the place and saw him, passed by on the other side. 33 But a Samaritan, as he traveled, came where the man was; and when he saw him, he took pity on him. 34 He went to him and bandaged his wounds, pouring on oil and wine. Then he put the man on his own donkey, brought him to an inn and took care of him. 35 The next day he took out two denarii and gave them to the innkeeper. 'Look after him,' he said, 'and when I return, I will reimburse you for any extra expense you may have.'

³⁶ "Which of these three do you think was a neighbor to the man who fell into the hands of robbers?"

³⁷ The expert in the law replied, "The one who had mercy on him." Jesus told him, "Go and do likewise."

REFLECT

The historical context of this well-known parable makes what Jesus is saying incredible radical. Although "love your neighbor as yourself" from Leviticus 19:18 summarized the Mosaic Law, Jesus redefines a neighbor to not only include a fellow Jew, but everyone. Jesus then not only includes a hated foreigner like the Samaritan, He makes him the hero and example to follow.[29]

There is another character in this story besides the Samaritan, priest, Levite, the man who was assaulted, and the innkeeper. Reread Luke 10:30-37. Can you identify the other characters referenced in the parable? Are they loved by God and created in His image? Do you struggle, as I do, to assign worth and value to The Humans who are seemingly cruel, heartless, and bent on doing evil?

PRAY

The only way to move abstract beliefs to core ones is to think, be honest, and give yourself grace. Who in your life or sphere of influence are like the band of robbers in the story of the Good Samaritan? Who do you struggle to see the image of God in or perhaps any other redeeming quality? Is it the unemployed beggar you pass on your way to work? Someone in your office who talks too loudly, knows too much, and drives you crazy?

---

[29] NIV Study Bible, 1558.

Perhaps your childhood was like mine and you were an innocent victim of someone else's advances or abuse. Take one minute and ask God what He wants to say to you about the band of robbers in your life. Of course, these are not easy abstract beliefs that will be addressed in one sitting with God. Let this serve as a starting point to begin looking for what God wants to free you from or show you, as always, in His love.

CHAPTER SIX:
YOUR SOMETHING

"... your faith is growing more and more, and the love
every one of you has for each other is increasing."
2 Thessalonians 1:3b

Even after serving in the inner city closely, frequently, and intentionally for the past eighteen months, I recently passed a homeless man on a bench while vacationing with my family in Phoenix over spring break and walked by, conflicted. I avoided a man at a gas station walking from car to car asking for money (I assumed) near my son's soon-to-be-college. The loud kids at Foley's high school, the speechless, scary man at Hope Street, and the homeless couple near my house—all people and situations I would have thought by now I would have organic and immediate responses to, but I do not. I do not because *doing something* is difficult, risky, and uncomfortable. Doing something and even an awareness of something is never easy.

I meet so many women who have a desire to do something to help others but are not sure where, how, or what something looks like. I thought helping at Hope Street would help make my response to someone like Indy, the man in Phoenix, or the man at the gas station easier and more instantaneous, but it has not. However, doing something has done something. Something is not magical or formulaic. Listening to God and allowing our abstract beliefs to become core ones takes time, but doing something is about doing, not perfection. Something means starting, failing, and getting back up. Doing something is about moving along a continuum in our hearts, homes, and heads and with the homeless, all the while observing, listening, and praying. When we expect something to look perfect, eloquent, and easy, we never do anything, because doing something is rarely any of those things.

So, what should your something look like? Where can you begin doing something?

· · · ·

Heart

"For this very reason, make every effort to add to your faith goodness; and to goodness, knowledge; and to knowledge, self-control; and to self-control, perseverance; and to perseverance, godliness; and to godliness, brotherly kindness; and to brotherly kindness, love. For if you possess these qualities in increasing measure, they will keep you from being ineffective and unproductive in your knowledge of our LORD Jesus Christ." 2 Peter 1:5-8

I once heard a speaker talk about measuring personal progress like a chart or graph, and I loved a concrete way to visualize growth. God is always moving us, as on a chart demarking progress, an increase of production, or a financial gain, "Up and To the Right," in Christ's likeness (Romans 8:29).

Moving Up and To the Right is never a straight line of perfect progress, but that does not negate our upward advancement. So, beginning with our hearts, how do we cooperate with the Spirit in moving us Up and To the Right? What is the something we can do in our hearts to begin walking alongside the homeless more frequently than we walk away from them?

Move Up and To the Right in His Word. What is the best way to ensure we are hearing from God and allowing Him to create the pure hearts in us that we need in our homes and with the homeless? Solomon says, "For the Lord gives wisdom and from his mouth come knowledge and understanding" (Proverbs 2:6). What does doing something in our hearts look like? Letting wisdom in: "For wisdom will enter your heart and knowledge will be pleasant to your soul. Discretion will protect you and understanding will guard you" (Proverbs 2:10-11).

Many of us read the Bible, attend weekly or bimonthly Bible studies, and believe God's Word to be inerrant and divinely inspired. Can we read the Bible, even occasionally or casually, and be transformed by it? I believe we can, because when I was a new Christian, that was my experience. The Bible was new to me, and as a busy mom, I would learn about and read it when I could. God's Word helped me in my parenting, marriage, and, most significantly, with my lifelong battle with anxiety. However, we are prone to complacency. We often eventually do not continue to allow the Spirit to take us deeper. Often we do not make the time or mental space to continue in God's Word.

The author of Hebrews warns against this and provides the remedy for the believer who settles for a casual and occasional relationship with God and the Bible: "In fact, though by this time you ought to be teachers, you need someone to teach you the elementary truths of God's word all over again. You need milk, not solid food! Anyone who lives on milk, being still an infant, is not acquainted with the teaching about righteousness. But solid food is for the mature, who by constant use have trained themselves to distinguish good and evil" (Hebrews 5:12-14).

Constant use and studying the book of Luke helped move me out of the comfortable and apathetic relationship with God's Word I had allowed myself to drift into. My longtime desire to *want* to read God's Word is finally happening more often only after twenty years of reading it because I should. Nothing about my study of the book of Luke was different or inspiring. However, reading and studying God's Word more deeply and slowly allowed the Spirit to begin to do His work. Abstractly I want to be moving Up and To the Right all the time and we ". . . are being transformed into his likeness with ever-increasing glory, which comes from the Lord, who is the Spirit" (2 Corinthians 3:18), but our response to the Spirit matters.

What does this something look like practically in our hearts? Continuing in the often mundane, difficult, and confusing work of getting into God's Word. It is only there we can learn to hear His voice and begin to discern what *something* looks like for us. It is only in the Bible we can confirm God's voice and allow the eyes of our hearts to be opened and reopened to the things of God.

To PONDER: What is difficult about making time to be in God's Word daily? Are you willing to ask God for a week (or a month) to help remove, rearrange, or reframe that difficulty?

. . . .

HOME

"Therefore, as God's chosen people, holy and dearly loved, clothe yourselves with compassion, kindness, humility, gentleness and patience." Colossians 3:12

What does something in your home look like practically? In my home, God, in His grace and love, has helped me in my marriage a great deal since the Black Friday Incident of 2013. He has helped by answering a prayer I have prayed almost daily for years by providing me with opportunities. When I started getting busier with my speaking ministry, I would ask God every morning to keep me humble without humiliating me. However, because God does not compartmentalize life and faith, the answer to my prayer did not manifest itself in the spotlight of public speaking but where I was the most prideful. God gave me opportunities to clothe myself with humility where I least wanted it: parenting with my husband.

Not long after the Black Friday debacle, I was venting to my husband about one of my teenagers' inability to keep curfew. I am a firm believer in only making rules you are going to ensure are being followed. I knew said child was coming home five minutes late to be passive aggressive, so I needed to give her a consequence. For two decades of parenting, the unspoken understanding Chris and I had was when I vented to him, his job was to listen and side with me.

Not this time, however. This time he gently, lovingly, and probably very apprehensively told me how he felt when our kids were small. If I was going to leave for the night, I would leave Chris very specific, lengthy instructions including bedtimes. When I would return, I would ask for a rundown of the night including when the kids went to sleep. My husband shared how difficult it was when bedtime occurred at 8:38, despite his best efforts to get them in bed by my mandated time of 8:30. He told me how stressful, difficult, and unrealistic my rules often were. He reminded me that our teenager was a good kid. She was not partying or vandalizing things in the three minutes she was sometimes late.

Doing something in my home has looked like seeing and capitalizing on the countless difficult opportunities God and life provide me to practice humility, silence, and introspection repeatedly in my marriage and parenting. It is embarrassing to admit that my husband and children were and sometimes still are afraid to correct, confront, or question me. It is difficult to see how much my fear, control issues, and struggles with my self-esteem have adversely impacted my home. Doing something in our home is the most unflattering and undesirable something we can do, but I believe we must do something here before we do something anywhere else.

What does something look like in your home? Usually only you and the people you live with can answer that question. When we prayerfully discern what needs our attention at home before we go anywhere else, we must be prepared to look for and act upon opportunities—difficult opportunities, such as avoiding correcting our spouse, resisting doing for our children what they can do for themselves, and identifying and releasing our idols. God, in His love, will give us opportunity to do what we do not want and wish we could do well once and then move on. However, until we do some somethings in our home with the people we love the most, doing something outside our home can quickly become an escape, avoidance, or worse.

> To Ponder: What repeated frustration do you have with someone in your family or home? Will you ask God to show you something about the only part you can change and are responsible for—your part?

· · · ·

HEAD

"Do not conform any longer to the pattern of this world, but be transformed by the renewing of your mind. Then you will be able to test and approve what God's will is— his good, pleasing and perfect will." Romans 12:2

What is something we can do to help the homeless? When I was praying about sharing my story with Ashley, I visited Hope Street's website and saw a "Volunteer" tab. I clicked on it, hoping to find the something I could do, but one of the options suggested reading a book. I quickly dismissed that as too easy and inefficient. I wanted to really help, quickly and tangibly. However, looking back, I realize the best something I could have done to be more effective, engaged, and authentic in serving the homeless in Jesus' name was to do something in and for my head.

I needed to learn what it meant to help people in a way that treated them with dignity and was not about making me feel better. I needed to be better informed about my own biases, prejudices, and fears and how those things affect what it looks like to walk alongside the homeless. I needed to read a book like Gregory Boyle's *Tattoos on the Heart* to learn that seeing and understanding myself better affects how I see and treat others. When we are able to deal with our own insecurities, misperceptions and disappointments in ourselves, there is a shift in our core beliefs that starts to transcend people's social and economic status, skin color, and their success or failures.

Another something my head needed was to practice a concept I had learned in college but had forgotten: metacognition. I needed to think more about my thinking. Doing something for the homeless really started when the Holy Spirit allowed me to begin hearing myself. Sometimes doing something is merely listening to how sarcastic, negative, or judgmental we have gotten, in my case the demeaning tone I used with my husband. Had I not thought about my thinking, I would not have understood the impact my many idols were having on my life. The first something I needed to do was listen to the Holy Spirit and allow Him to renew my thinking. It sounds simple and easy, but we are busy, distracted, and tired. Sometimes doing something for the homeless is as basic and difficult as being still long enough to quiet the voices and noise in our heads, noise that so easily overshadows hearing ourselves and hearing God.

To Ponder: Do you have any time in your day to just be, or are you always on your phone, checking email and social media, or on the run? At what time of day every day could you consistently make one minute to pray and think about your thinking?

. . . .

The Homeless

"'I am the Lord's servant,' Mary answered, 'May it be to me as you have said.'" Luke 1:38a

I have a friend who has adopted five Chinese children, all with health issues. I have another friend who attends and volunteers at Special Olympic events in our area. In addition to Foley, we have for the last two years hosted international high school students. Our Italian/Asian family looks something like the League of Nations when we go to the park with Foley and whatever international student happens to be living with us on any given day.

Something looks different for everyone, and so does our call to something beyond ourselves, in Jesus' name.

In Luke 1:26-38, the angel Gabriel visits Mary to tell her she is being called to something. It appears Mary has been faithful with the somethings in her heart, home, and mind because Gabriel says she is "highly favored" (vs. 28). Mary is not flattered by this comment but is wisely cautious and asks him some questions about this something. We think we want the Lord to speak to us like Gabriel came to Mary, but it is interesting that Mary has her questions and doubts even with this divine, supernatural delivery of what her something was supposed to be. Gabriel's answer to Mary's questions and trepidation is to tell her about Jesus: His name, supreme authority, and eternal power. After another question, Mary finally surrenders to her something saying, "I am the Lord's servant . . ." (vs. 38a).

Surrendering to something comes down to two things: our

willingness to be a servant and who Christ is to us. It goes back to a personal encounter with the Lord like Mary's where we recognize fear, raise questions, and remember God's power. Where is God meeting you in the silence of your everyday and calling you to greater purpose and things that matter for eternity? It may, and will more than likely, take you years, if you are like me, to hear the call clearly to something you possibly never imagined. Mary discovered surrendering to the status of servant comes with a cost, and although our call and cost will pale to her call, there are hard lessons and great sacrifices when we surrender to the Spirit.

I remember hearing a sermon once where the pastor had a long, long rope that extended the length of the stage. The rope was probably forty feet long, and in the middle of it, the pastor had wrapped a piece of tape. He said the small fraction of tape represented our lives and the rope represented eternity. I live most of my life worried about that quarter of an inch. By and large, I forget and ignore the truth of eternity and focus only on the tiny microscopic speck this life comprises on the spectrum of forever. I do not want to miss my greater callings from the Lord and certainly do not want to refuse them. Walking by the homeless has helped me to begin living the abundant life Christ came to give me beyond the quarter inch of this life.

What is your greater calling to impact eternity? Keep recognizing places you are afraid, raising questions you have, and remembering God's power, because although the cost of surrender is high, the rewards are eternal.

> "...although the cost of surrender is high, the rewards are eternal."

To Ponder: Share the last time you thought about heaven and the life after this one. What were your thoughts, fears, questions, and ponderings?

••••

Chapter Six:
Your Something —
Putting It All Together

Read Luke 1:26-38

26 In the sixth month of Elizabeth's pregnancy, God sent the angel Gabriel to Nazareth, a town in Galilee, 27 to a virgin pledged to be married to a man named Joseph, a descendant of David. The virgin's name was Mary. 28 The angel went to her and said, "Greetings, you who are highly favored! The Lord is with you."

29 Mary was greatly troubled at his words and wondered what kind of greeting this might be. 30 But the angel said to her, "Do not be afraid, Mary; you have found favor with God. 31 You will conceive and give birth to a son, and you are to call him Jesus. 32 He will be great and will be called the Son of the Most High. The Lord God will give him the throne of his father David, 33 and he will reign over Jacob's descendants forever; his kingdom will never end."

34 "How will this be," Mary asked the angel, "since I am a virgin?"

35 The angel answered, "The Holy Spirit will come on you, and the power of the Most High will overshadow you. So the holy one to be born will be called the Son of God. 36 Even Elizabeth your relative is going to have a child in her old age, and she who was said to be unable to conceive is in her sixth month. 37 For no word from God will ever fail."

38 "I am the Lord's servant," Mary answered. "May your word to me be fulfilled." Then the angel left her.

REFLECT

Which matters more to you, to be seen by God as highly favored or to do great things for Him? For me, it is definitely doing great things for Him. Being highly favored means dying to myself, clothing myself with things like compassion and forgiveness. It means surrendering things I like and want to hold onto. Doing great things, on the other hand, just sounds so . . . great.

Part of my current moving "Up and To the Right" journey is trying to overcome my lifelong quest to be a people pleaser. I am learning in a discipleship group that I am in that part of the reason I want to do great things is to prove my value and worth. Pleasing people gives me a measurable and visible way to assess whether I am good, smart, and pretty enough. Right, wrong, or indifferent, therefore, I base my identity and worth in people, not in Christ. It is not a core belief that I am the daughter of the Most-High God. It sounds nice, and I believe it for others, but not for myself.

I have been processing, praying, and reading Scripture about this daily for over seven months. I have been what our group facilitator calls "sitting in my weeds," that is, residing for months in the uncomfortable place of learning hard things about myself, being still, and observing where God is at work in my life. What have I learned in seven months? Not as much as I would like. Despite many ah-ha moments, I am still actively waiting to look different. I am still threatened by beautiful, intelligent, and confident women. I am still afraid you will not like this book and will criticize it. I worry my husband will grow tired of me.

I am still sitting in my weeds.

> "...being uncomfortable is always better than being unchanged."

I do not want to sit in my, yours, or anyone else's weeds. I do not want to "hold my cactus" or any other horrible euphemism depicting the uncomfortable learning and waiting process when God helps us with our problems, issues, and places of bondage. But my journey—learning to see myself as God does—is just like my journey walking by the homeless. It is slow, painful, and unpleasant, but, thankfully, we do not stay in the weeds forever. The weeds are not an end to themselves.

Are we willing to be still, listen, and persevere in the places God wants to free us and change us? We cannot rush into a desire to help the poor, love The Humans, or be the wife we wish we were. The Christian life is a lot of cactus-holding, but being uncomfortable is always better than being unchanged. Being sanctified is always better than being stagnant. We must remember that in the weeds and cactuses that make up most of our ordinary lives, "What we call the process God calls the end."[30] Knowing God's love more deeply and in a way that changes us is worth every struggle, and that love must be the basis and root of doing something, in Jesus' name.

PRAY

One of my homework assignments in my discipleship group was to take time to enjoy God. I had no idea what that meant. I knew, however, that it sounded unproductive and, therefore,

---

[30] Chambers, July 28th.

unappealing. I tried enjoying God (because I had to) many times and in many ways for weeks. This was contrived and confusing. However, after several months, attempts, and some practice, I have come to the place where I can just enjoy being with God.

Part of what makes sitting in our weeds tolerable is that we are not just sitting. Waiting on God never looks like being curled up in the fetal position, motionless and lifeless. It is active waiting. It is actively waiting, watching, and listening in the arduous and uncomfortable places God takes us. When we actively wait on God, He always, always eventually shows us His deep love for us in a personal and intimate way.

Take a walk, go for a bike ride, weed your garden. Do whatever it does that brings you joy where you might be able to see, feel, and hear God. Do not pray or confess anything, just be with God for at least ten minutes. If you are like me and that is not only hard for you, it is horrible, just keep trying it. Once it becomes less horrible or even wonderful, pray for part of your time with Jesus and ask Him what *something* looks like for you and then just listen . . .

ACKNOWLEDGMENTS

"When Moses' hands grew tired, they took a stone and put it under him and he sat on it. Aaron and Hur held his hands up – one on one side, one on the other – so that his hands remained steady till sunset." Exodus 17:12

There were many people who genuinely held me up amid all the details and challenges that accompanied the writing of this book. Thank you to the following for co-authoring *Walking By the Homeless:*

- To my family for allowing me to be holed up in my office, on vacation, and when I should have been feeding you. Thank you, Hannah, for being a great sounding board; Casey, for proudly telling your teachers that your mom wrote a book; and Faithe, for telling me I should be proud of myself for this accomplishment. Chris, the fact that you can't wait for my next book after all this one cost you in time, work, and energy talking me off the ledge multiple times proves you are what I've always said, a saint I don't deserve. I love you guys.
- To my prayer team, Chrissy, Kim, Jenny, Marlene, Patricia, and Aimee. Thank you for every text and email

and for covering every prayer request in detail. I love each of you and thank you for giving generously of your time and concern and for your passion for the power of prayer. A special thank you to Aimee for your constant, specific, and timely encouragements and for delivering me chocolate when I wanted to quit. You are this Asian Hillbilly's favorite Swedish Girl . . .

- To Pops. You have been Foley's constant and steady. You have given him more love and support than anyone else. You are strong, wise, and steadfast, and your heart for the young men you have raised is simply amazing. We are forever grateful you are in Foley's and our lives.

- To Judge Foley. Thank you for stepping out so bravely and in obedience to find Foley (and hundreds of other children) a forever family. You are a wonderful, kind, and selfless human being, friend, and servant.

- To my Hope Street family. I love you. Thank you, Ash, for praying for me when you didn't know why you were supposed to and for your incredible heart for the Lord and the city of Milwaukee.

- To Shelly. Thank you for talking me out of throwing my computer out the window a few months before I wrote *Walking By the Homeless*. Thank you for telling me writing is hard work, for being an encourager but never a flatterer, and for your timely quotes and emails, always spurring me on.

- To the team at Orange Hat Publishing. Shannon, you are now, more than ever, my Asian sister. Thank you for planting the seed for this so many years ago and for your genuine, heartfelt, and epic smile. Never lose it. Carolyn, your patience, wisdom, and attention to detail are gifts. Thank you for making me better and for never giving up on me and my inability to use and understand basic technology. You are not just an editor but an amazing encourager, communicator, and teacher.

- To Emmie. Thank you for making this book look so beautiful. You made the vision I had for the cover even more than I could have asked for or imagined. Thank you for sharing my heart for Christ and for the homeless. Love you, friend!

- To Leslee, Jeff, and Mary. Thank you for your help in the eleventh hour with so many final details. Your willingness to help (and on such short notice) was so appreciated. Thank you, most of all, for your servant hearts that love people and the Lord deeply, authentically, and selflessly. Love you, friends!

- To the Holy Spirit. There are times I reread things in this book that I have no recollection of writing—so indicative of the Spirit's work through and despite me. Thank you, Father, for being in all of this and letting me just be a small part.

BIBLIOGRAPHY

Barnett, Paul. *The Message of 2 Corinthians*. Downers Grove, IL: InterVarsity Press, 1988.

Boyle, Gregory. *Tattoos on the Heart*. New York City, NY: Free Press, 2010.

Bromiley, Geoffrey W. *Theological Dictionary of the New Testament*. Grand Rapids, MI: William B. Eerdmans Publishing Company, 1985.

Chambers, Oswald. *My Utmost for His Highest*. Uhrichsville, OH: Barbour Publishing, Inc., 1963.

Erickson, Millard J. *Christian Theology*. Grand Rapids, MI: Baker Academic, 2006.

John H. Walton, Victor H. Matthews, Mark W. Chavalas. *The IVP Bible Background Commentary: Old Testament*. Downers Grove, IL: InterVarsity Press, 2014.

Keller, Timothy. *Preaching*. New York, NY: Penguin Books, 2016.

Kohlenberger, John R. *Zondervan NIV Nave's Topical Bible*. Grand Rapids, MI: Zondervan, 1994.

Ortberg, John. *The Life You've Always Wanted*. Grand Rapids, MI: Zondervan, 2002.

Osborne, Grant R. *Romans*. Downers Grove, IL: InterVarsity Press, 2004.

The NIV Study Bible. Grand Rapids, MI: Zondervan, 1984.

Wright, N.T. *John For Everyone Part 2*. Louisville, KY: John Knox Press, 2004.

ABOUT THE AUTHOR

Laura is a former high school teacher, stay-at-home mom, and ministry director. She graduated from Trinity Evangelical Divinity School with her master's degree in Theological Studies at the tender age of forty-eight. She has been married to her husband Chris for twenty-six years, and they have three children: Hannah, Casey, and Faithe. Chris and Laura love taking walks together, being with their children whenever possible, and share a deep love of coffee.

Made in the USA
Lexington, KY
08 December 2018